2nd Workshop on Computational Approaches to Linguistic Creativity 2010

Held at NAACL HLT 2010

Los Angeles, California, USA
5 June 2010

ISBN: 978-1-61738-672-5

Printed from e-media with permission by:

Curran Associates, Inc.
57 Morehouse Lane
Red Hook, NY 12571

Some format issues inherent in the e-media version may also appear in this print version.

Printed by Curran Associates, Inc. (2010)

For permission requests, please contact the Association for Computational Linguistics at the address below.

Association for Computational Linguistics
209 N. Eighth Street
Stroudsburg, Pennsylvania 18360

Phone: 1-570-476-8006
Fax: 1-570-476-0860

acl@aclweb.org

Additional copies of this publication are available from:

Curran Associates, Inc.
57 Morehouse Lane
Red Hook, NY 12571 USA
Phone: 845-758-0400
Fax: 845-758-2634
Email: curran@proceedings.com
Web: www.proceedings.com

Introduction

It is generally agreed upon that creativity is an important property of human language. For example, speakers routinely coin new words, employ novel metaphors, and play with words through puns. Indeed, such creative processes take place at all levels of language from the lexicon, to syntax, semantics, and discourse. Creativity allows speakers to express themselves with their own individual style. It further provides new ways of looking at the world, by describing something through the use of unusual comparisons for effect or emphasis, and thus making language more engaging and fun. Listeners are typically able to understand creative language without any difficulties. On the other hand, generating and recognizing creative language presents a tremendous challenge for natural language processing (NLP) systems.

The recognition of instances of linguistic creativity, and the computation of their meaning, constitute one of the most challenging problems for a variety of NLP tasks, such as machine translation, text summarization, information retrieval, dialog systems, and sentiment analysis. Moreover, models of linguistic creativity are necessary for systems capable of generating story narratives, jokes, or poetry. Nevertheless, despite the importance of linguistic creativity in many NLP tasks, it still remains unclear how to model, simulate, or evaluate linguistic creativity. Furthermore, research on topics related to linguistic creativity has not received a great deal of attention at major computational linguistics conferences in recent years.

CALC-09 was the first venue to present research on a wide range of topics related to linguistic creativity including computational models of metaphor, generation of creative texts, and measuring morphological and constructional productivity. CALC-10 is the continuation of our efforts to provide a venue for research on all aspects and modalities of linguistic creativity.

For CALC-10, we received a total of nine submissions. Six papers were accepted for oral presentation. The topics range from understanding to generating creative language to tools for creative writing. We are especially grateful to the authors who submitted excellent papers and to our hard working program committee. We would like to express our enormous gratitude to the U.S. National Science Foundation (IIS award #: 0906244) for the support of the workshop which allowed us to invite Pablo Gervás to give a keynote talk, and whose paper is included in this volume. Pablo Gervás is Associate Professor of Electrical Engineering and Artificial Intelligence at The Complutense University of Madrid. In his paper, he reviews recent research and implementation efforts in computational creativity, automated story telling, and poetry generation, exploring how the computational models relate to human performance. Last but not least, we want to thank Claudia Leacock and Richard Wicentowski, the publication chairs.

Paul Cook and Anna Feldman

Organizers:

Paul Cook, University of Toronto (Canada)
Anna Feldman, Montclair State University (USA)

Program Committee:

Kirk Baker, Collexis, Washington, DC (USA)
Roberto Basili, University of Roma (Italy)
Beata Beigman Klebanov, Northwestern University (USA)
Amilcar Cardoso, Coimbra (Portugal)
Mona Diab, Columbia University (USA)
Afsaneh Fazly, Shiraz University (Iran)
Eileen Fitzpatrick, Montclair State University (USA)
Pablo Gervás, Universidad Complutense de Madrid (Spain)
Roxana Girju, University of Illinois at Urbana-Champaign (USA)
Sid Horton, Northwestern University (USA)
Diana Inkpen, University of Ottawa (Canada)
Mark Lee, University of Birmingham (UK)
Birte Lönneker-Rodman, Across Systems GmbH (Germany)
Xiaofei Lu, Penn State University (USA)
Ruli Manurung, University of Indonesia (Indonesia)
Katja Markert, University of Leeds (UK)
Saif Mohammad, National Research Council, Ottawa (Canada)
Anton Nijholt, Twente (The Netherlands)
Ted Pedersen, University of Minnesota in Duluth (USA)
Vasile Rus, The University of Memphis (USA)
Gerard Steen, Vrije Universiteit (The Netherlands)
Juergen Trouvain, Saarland University (Germany)

Invited Speaker:

Pablo Gervás, Universidad Complutense de Madrid (Spain)

Table of Contents

Workshop Program

Saturday, June 5, 2010

1:30–1:45	Opening remarks
	Understanding creative language
1:45–2:10	*Automatic conjugation and identification of regular and irregular verb neologisms in Spanish* Luz Rello and Eduardo Basterrechea
2:10–2:35	*Mining and Classification of Neologisms in Persian Blogs* Karine Megerdoomian and Ali Hadjarian
2:35–3:00	*Comparing Semantic Role Labeling with Typed Dependency Parsing in Computational Metaphor Identification* Eric P. S. Baumer, James P. White and Bill Tomlinson
3:00–3:30	**Break**
	Invited talk
3:00–4:30	*Engineering Linguistic Creativity: Bird Flight and Jet Planes* Pablo Gervás
4:30–4:40	**Break**
	Generating creative language
4:40–5:05	*An alternate approach towards meaningful lyric generation in Tamil* Ananth Ramakrishnan A and Sobha Lalitha Devi
5:05–5:30	*Representing Story Plans in SUMO* Jeffrey Cua, Ruli Manurung, Ethel Ong and Adam Pease
5:30–5:55	*Computational Creativity Tools for Songwriters* Burr Settles
5:55–6:00	Closing remarks

Automatic conjugation and identification of regular and irregular verb neologisms in Spanish

Luz Rello and Eduardo Basterrechea
Molino de Ideas s.a.
Nanclares de Oca, 1F
Madrid, 28022, Spain
{lrello, ebaste}@molinodeideas.es

Abstract

In this paper, a novel system for the automatic identification and conjugation of Spanish verb neologisms is presented. The paper describes a rule-based algorithm consisting of six steps which are taken to determine whether a new verb is regular or not, and to establish the rules that the verb should follow in its conjugation. The method was evaluated on 4,307 new verbs and its performance found to be satisfactory both for irregular and regular neologisms. The algorithm also contains extra rules to cater for verb neologisms in Spanish that do not exist as yet, but are inferred to be possible in light of existing cases of new verb creation in Spanish.

1 Introduction

This paper presents a new method consisting of a set of modules which are implemented as part of a free online conjugator called *Onoma*[1].

The novelty of this system lies in its ability to identify and conjugate existing verbs and potential new verbs in Spanish with a degree of coverage that cannot completely be achieved by other existing conjugators that are available. Other existing systems do not cope well with the productively rich word formation processes that apply to Spanish verbs and lead to complexities in their inflectional forms that can present irregularities. The operation of these processes mean that each Spanish verb can comprise 135 different forms, including compound verb forms.

Several researchers have developed tools and methods related to Spanish verbs. These include morphological processors (Tzoukermann and Liberman, 1990), (Santana et al., 1997), (Santana et al., 2002), semantic verb classification (Esteve Ferrer, 2004) or verb sense disambiguation (Lapata and Brew, 2004). Nevertheless, to our knowledge, ours is the first attempt to automatically identify, classify and conjugate new Spanish verbs.

Our method identifies new and existing Spanish verbs and categorises them into seven classes: one class for regular verbs and six classes of irregular verbs depending on the type of the irregularity rule whose operation produced it. This algorithm is implemented by means of six modules or transducers which process each new infinitive form and classify the neologism. Once the new infinitive is classified, it is conjugated by the system using a set of high accuracy conjugation rules according to its class.

One of the advantages of this procedure is that only very little information about the new infinitive form is required. The knowledge needed is exclusively of a formal kind. Extraction of this information relies on the implementation and use of two extra modules: one to detect Spanish syllables, and the other to split the verb into its root and morphological affixes.

In cases where the neologism is not an infinitive form, but a conjugated one, the system generates a hypothetical infinitive form that the user can corroborate as a legitimate infinitive.

Given that the transducers used in this system are easy to learn and remember, the method can be employed as a pedagogic tool itself by students of

[1] *Onoma* can be accessed at http://conjugador.onoma.es

Proceedings of the NAACL HLT 2010 Second Workshop on Computational Approaches to Linguistic Creativity, pages 1–5,
Los Angeles, California, June 2010.

Spanish as a foreign language. It helps in the learning of the Spanish verb system since currently existing methods (e.g. (Puebla, 1995), (Gomis, 1998), (Mateo, 2008)) do not provide guidance on the question of whether verbs are regular or irregular. This is due to the fact that our method can identify the nature of any possible verb by reference only to its infinitive form. The application of other kinds of knowledge about the verb to this task are currently being investigated to deal with those rare cases in which reference to the infinitive form is insufficient for making this classification.

This study first required an analysis of the existing verb paradigms used in dictionary construction (DRAE, 2001) followed by the detailed examination of new verbs' conjugations (Gomis, 1998), (Santana et al., 2002), (Mateo, 2008) compiled in a database created for that purpose. For the design of the algorithm, in order to validate the rules and patterns, an error-driven approach was taken.

The remainder of the paper is structured as follows: section 2 presents a description of the corpora used. In Section 3, the different word formation processes that apply to Spanish verbs are described, while Section 4 is devoted to the detailed description of the rules used by the system to classify the neologisms, which are evaluated in Section 5. Finally, in Section 6 we draw the conclusions.

2 Data

Two databases were used for the modeling process. The first (named the DRAE Verb Conjugation Database (DRAEVC-DB)) is composed of all the paradigms of the verbs contained in the 22nd edition of the Dictionary of the Royal Spanish Academy (DRAE, 2001). This database contains 11,060 existing Spanish verbs and their respective conjugations. The second database (named the MolinoIdeas Verb Conjugation Database (MIVC-DB)), created for this purpose, contains 15,367 verbs. It includes all the verbs found in the DRAE database plus 4,307 conjugated Spanish verbs that are not registered in the Royal Spanish Academy Dictionary (DRAE, 2001), which are found in standard and colloquial Spanish and whose use is frequent on the web.

The MIVC-DB contains completely conjugated verbs occurring in the Spanish Wikipedia and in a collection of 3 million journalistic articles from newspapers in Spanish from America and Spain[2].

Corpus	Number of verbs
DRAE	11,060
MolinoIdeas	15,367

Table 1: Corpora used.

Verbs which do not occur in the Dictionary of the Royal Spanish Academy (DRAE, 2001) are considered neologisms in this study. Thus 4,307 of the 15,367 verbs in the MIVC-DB are neologisms. The paradigms of the new verbs whose complete conjugation was not found in the sources were automatically computed and manually revised in order to ensure their accuracy. The result of this semi-automatic process is a database consisting only of attested Spanish verbs.

3 Creativity in Spanish verbs

The creation of new verbs in Spanish is especially productive due to the rich possibilities of the diverse morphological schema that are applied to create neologisms (Almela, 1999).

New Spanish verbs are derived by two means: either (1) morphological processes applied to existing words or (2) incorporating foreign verbs, such as *digitalizar* from *to digitalize*.

Three morphological mechanisms can be distinguished: prefixation, suffixation and parasynthesis. Through prefixation a bound morpheme is attached to a previously existing verb. The most common prefixes used for new verbs found in our corpus are the following: *a- (abastillar), des- (desagrupar), inter- (interactuar), pre- (prefabricar), re- (redecorar), sobre- (sobretasar), sub- (subvaluar)* and *super- (superdotar)*. On the other hand, the most frequent suffixes in Spanish new verbs are *-ar (palar), -ear (panear), -ificar (cronificar)* and *-izar (superficializar)*. Finally, parasynthesis occurs when the suffixes are added in combination with a prefix (bound morpheme). Although parasynthesis is rare in other grammatical classes, it is quite relevant in the creation of new Spanish verbs (Serrano,

[2]The newspapers with mayor representation in our corpus are: *El País, ABC, Marca, Público, El Universal, Clarín, El Mundo* and *El Norte de Castilla*

1999). The most common prefixes are *-a* or *-en* in conjunction with the suffixes *-ar, -ear, -ecer* and *-izar* (*acuchillear, enmarronar, enlanguidecer, abandalizar*).

In this paper, the term derivational base is used to denote the immediate constituent to which a morphological process is applied to form a verb. In order to obtain the derivational base, it is necessary to determine whether the last vowel of the base is stressed. When the vowel is unstressed, it is removed from the derivational base while a stressed vowel remains as part of the derivational base. If a consonant is the final letter of the derivational base it remains a part of it as well.

4 Classifying and conjugating new verbs

Broadly speaking, the algorithm is implemented by six transduction modules arranged in a switch structure. The operation of most of the transducers is simple, though Module 4 is implemented as a cascade of transduction modules in which inputs may potentially be further modified by subsequent modules (5 and 6).

The modules were implemented to determine the class of each neologism. Depending on the class to which each verb belongs, a set of rules and patterns will be applied to create its inflected forms. The proposed verb taxonomy generated by these transducers is original and was developed in conjunction with the method itself. The group of patterns and rules which affect each verb are detailed in previous work (Basterrechea and Rello, 2010). The modules described below are activated when they receive as input an existing or new infinitive verb form. When the infinitive form is not changed by one transducer, it is tested against the next one. If not adjusted by any transducer, then the new infinitive verb is assumed to have a regular conjugation.

Module 1: The first transducer checks whether the verb form is an auxiliary verb (*haber*), a copulative verb (*ser* or *estar*), a monosyllabic verb (*ir*, *dar* or *ver*), a Magnificent verb[3], or a prefixed form whose derivational base matches one of these aforementioned types of verbs. If the form matches one of these cases, the verb is irregular and will undergo the rules and patterns of its own class. (Basterrechea and Rello, 2010).

Module 2: If the infinitive or prefixed infinitive form finishes in *-quirir (adquirir)* or belongs to the list: *dormir, errar, morir, oler, erguir* or *desosar*, the form is recognized as an irregular verb and will be conjugated using the irregularity rules which operate on the root vowel, which can be either diphthongized or replaced by another vowel (*adquiero* from *adquirir*, *duermo* and *durmió* from *dormir*).

Module 3: The third transducer identifies whether the infinitive form root ends in a vowel. If the verb belongs to the second or third conjugation (*-er* and *-ir* endings) (*leer, oír*), it is an irregular verb, while if the verb belongs to the first conjugation (*-ar* ending) then it will only be irregular if its root ends with an *-u* or *-i* (*criar, actuar*). For the verbs assigned to the first conjugation, diacritic transduction rules are applied to their inflected forms (*crío* from *criar*, *actúo* from *actuar*); in the case of verbs assigned to the second and third conjugations, the alterations performed on their inflected forms are mainly additions or subtitutions of letters (*leyó* de *leer*, *oigo* de *oír*).

There are some endings such as (*-ier*, *-uer* and *-iir*) which are not found in the MIVC-DB. In the hypothetical case where they are encountered, their conjugation would have followed the rules detailed earlier. Rules facilitating the conjugation of potential but non-existing verbs are included in the algorithm.

Module 4: When an infinitive root form in the first conjugation ends in *-c, -z, -g* or *-gu* (*secar*, *trazar*, *delegar*) and in the second and third conjugation ends in *-c, -g, -gu* or *-qu* (*conocer*, *corregir*, *seguir*), that verb is affected by consonantal orthographic adjustments (irregularity rules) in order to preserve its pronunciation (*sequé* from *secar*, *tracé* from *trazar*, *delegué* from *delegar*, *conozco* from *conocer*, *corrijo* from *corregir*, *sigo* from *seguir*).

In case the infinitive root form of the second and third conjugation ends in *-ñ* or *-ll* (*tañer*, *engullir*), the vowel *i* is removed from some endings of the paradigm following the pattern detailed in (Basterrechea and Rello, 2010).

Verbs undergoing transduction by Module 4 can undergo further modification by Modules 5 and 6. Any infinitive form which failed to meet the trig-

[3] There are 14 so-called Magnificent verbs: *traer, valer, salir, tener, venir, poner, hacer, decir, poder, querer, saber, caber, andar* and *-ducir* (Basterrechea and Rello, 2010).

gering conditions set by Modules 1-4 is also tested against 5 and 6.

Module 5: This module focuses on determining the vowel of the infinitive form root and the verb's derivational base. If the vowel is *e* or *o* in the first conjugation and the verb derivational base includes diphthongs *ie* or *ue* (*helar*, *contar*), or if the vowel is *e* in the infinitive forms belonging to the second and third conjugation (*servir*, *herir*), then the verb is irregular and it is modified by the irregularity rules which perform either a substitution of this vowel (*sirvo* from *servir*) or a diphthongization (*hielo* from *helar*, *cuento* from *contar* or *hiero* from *herir*).

Module 6: Finally, the existence of a diphthong in the infinitive root is examined (*reunir*, *europeizar*). If the infinitive matches the triggering condition for this transducer, its paradigm is considered irregular and the same irregularity rules from module 3 -inserting a written accent in certain inflected forms- are applied (*reúno* from *reunir*, *europeízo* from *europeizar*).

Any verb form that fails to meet the triggering conditions set by any of these six transducers has regular conjugation.

It is assumed that these 6 modules cover the full range of both existing and potential verbs in Spanish. The modules' reliability was tested using the full paradigms of 15,367 verbs. As noted earlier, there are some irregularity rules in module 3 which predict the irregularities of non existing but possible neologisms in Spanish. Those rules, in conjunction with the rest of the modules, cover the recognition and conjugation of the potential new verbs.

5 Evaluation

The transducers have been evaluated over all the verbs from the DRAEVC-DB and the 4,307 new verbs from MICV-DB.

In case a new verb appears which is not similar to the ones contained in our corpus, the transduction rules in Module 3 for non existing but potential verbs in Spanish would be activated, although no examples of that type have been encountered in the test data used here. As this system is part of the free online conjugator *Onoma*, it is constantly being evaluated on the basis of users' input.

Every time a new infinitive form absent from MIVC-DB is introduced by the user[4], it is automatically added to the database. The system is constantly updated since it is revised every time a new irregularity is detected by the algorithm. The goal is to enable future adaptation of the algorithm to newly encountered phenomena within the language. So far, non-normative verbs, invented by the users, such as *arreburbujear, insomniar, pizzicatear* have also been conjugated by *Onoma*.

Verb neologism type	**Verb neologism class**	**Number of neologisms**
regular	regular rules	3,154
irregular	module 1 rules	27
irregular	module 2 rules	9
irregular	module 3 rules	39
irregular	module 4 rules	945
irregular	module 5 rules	87
irregular	module 6 rules	46
Total verb neologisms		**4,307**

Table 2: New verbs evaluation

Of all the new verbs in MIVC-DB, 3,154 were regular and 1,153 irregular (see Table 2). The majority of the irregular neologisms were conjugated by transducer 4.

6 Conclusions

Creativity is a property of human language and the processing of instances of linguistic creativity represents one of the most challenging problems in NLP. Creative processes such as word formation affect Spanish verbs to a large extent: more than 50% of the actual verbs identified in the data set used to build MIVC-DB do not appear in the largest Spanish dictionary. The processing of these neologisms poses the added difficulty of their rich inflectional morphology which can be also irregular. Therefore, the automatic and accurate recognition and generation of new verbal paradigms is a substantial advance in neologism processing in Spanish.

In future work we plan to create other algorithms to treat the rest of the open-class grammatical categories and to identify and generate inflections of new

[4]Forms occurring due to typographical errors are not included.

words not prescribed by dictionaries.

Acknowledgments

We would like to express or gratitude to the Molino de Ideas s.a. engineering team who have successfully implemented the method, specially to Daniel Ayuso de Santos and Alejandro de Pablos López.

References

Ramón Almela Pérez. 1999. *Procedimientos de formación de palabras en español.* Ariel, Barcelona, España.

Eduardo Basterrechea and Luz Rello. 2010. *El verbo en español. Construye tu propio verbo.* Molino de Ideas, Madrid, España.

Eva Esteve Ferrer. 2004. Towards a semantic classification of Spanish verbs based on subcategorisation information. *Proceedings of the ACL 2004 workshop on Student research*, 13.

Pedro Gomis Blanco and Laura Segura. 1998. *Vademécum del verbo español.* SGEL. Sociedad General Española de Librería, Madrid, España.

Mirella Lapata and Chris Brew. 2004. Verb class disambiguation using informative priors. *Computational Linguistics*, 30(1): 45–73.

Francis Mateo. 2008. *Bescherelle. Les verbes espagnols.* Hatier, Paris, France.

Jorge Puebla Ortega. 1995. *Cómo conjugar todos los verbos del español.* Playor, Madrid, España.

Real Academia Española. 2001. *Diccionario de la lengua española*, 22 edición. Espasa, Madrid, España.

David Serrano Dolader. 1999. La derivación verbal y la parasíntesis. *Gramática descriptiva de la lengua española*, I. Bosque, V. Demonte, (eds.), (3): 4683-4756. Real Academia Española / Espasa, Madrid, España.

Evelyne Tzoukermann and Mark Y. Liberman. 1990. A Finite-State Morphological Processor for Spanish. *Proceedings of the 13th conference on Computational linguistics*, (1): 277-282.

Octavio Santana Suárez, José Rafael Pérez Aguiar, Zenón José Hernández Figueroa, Francisco Javier Carreras Riudavets, Gustavo Rodríguez Rodríguez. 1997. FLAVER: Flexionador y lematizador automático de formas verbales. *lingüística española actual XIX*, (2): 229-282. Arco Libros, Madrid, España.

Octavio Santana Suárez, Francisco Javier Carreras Riudavets, Zenón José Hernández Figueroa, José Rafael Pérez Aguiar and Gustavo Rodríguez Rodríguez. 2002. *Manual de la conjugacin del español. 12 790 verbos conjugados.* Arco Libros, Madrid, España.

Mining and Classification of Neologisms in Persian Blogs

Karine Megerdoomian
The MITRE Corporation
7515 Colshire Drive
McLean, VA 22102, USA
karine@mitre.org

Ali Hadjarian
The MITRE Corporation
7515 Colshire Drive
McLean, VA 22102, USA
ahadjarian@mitre.org

Abstract

The exponential growth of the Persian blogosphere and the increased number of neologisms create a major challenge in NLP applications of Persian blogs. This paper describes a method for extracting and classifying newly constructed words and borrowings from Persian blog posts. The analysis of the occurrence of neologisms across five distinct topic categories points to a correspondence between the topic domain and the type of neologism that is most commonly encountered. The results suggest that different approaches should be implemented for the automatic detection and processing of neologisms depending on the domain of application.

1 Introduction*

Since its beginnings in 2001, the Persian blogosphere has undergone a dramatic growth making Persian one of the top ten languages of the global blog community in 2007 [Sifry 2007].

One of the main challenges in the automatic analysis and processing of Persian language blogs is the accelerated emergence of neologisms in online discourse. These newly created words that cannot be found in traditional lexicons primarily consist of adopted English loanwords, such as دانلود *dânlod* 'download' or آنلاین *ânlâyn* 'online', and innovative constructions based on Persian word-formation principles, as in فیلترشکن *filtershekan* 'anti-filter software' or چتیدن *chatidan* 'to chat'.

In this paper, we investigate the distinct classes of neologisms encountered in Persian language blogs. Since the main goal of the project is to build a topic classification system for blogs, we focused on extracting neologisms that would have the most discriminatory power in distinguishing between the various classes.

For the purposes of this study, we collected a corpus of Persian language blogs from five different topic categories of sports, medicine, politics, Internet, and cinema. The neologisms are automatically extracted by running the documents through a morphological analyzer. Since these new word coinages are not recognized by the analyzer, they are tagged as unknowns. A weight-ordered list of unknown words is then generated for each topic category, using information gain as the measure, as described in Section 2.3. The more significant neologisms for each category are then manually identified from the generated weight-ordered lists, focusing on the top 200 words, and classified based on their linguistic characteristics. The results indicate that the type of neologism found in the blog posts in fact corresponds to the topic domain. Hence, for example, while English loans are highly prominent in technical and Internet related posts, new morphological constructions are more common in the domain of politics. Building on these results, we argue that distinct approaches are required for processing the adopted loan words and the morphologically constructed neologisms.

* This research is part of a larger project on the study of Persian language blogs supported by a Mission-Oriented Investigation and Experimentation (MOIE) program at MITRE.

Proceedings of the NAACL HLT 2010 Second Workshop on Computational Approaches to Linguistic Creativity, pages 6–13,
Los Angeles, California, June 2010. ©2010 Association for Computational Linguistics

2 Extraction Process

2.1 Blog Data

The blog data for this study comes from Blogfa[1], a popular Persian blog hosting site. The topic index provided by Blogfa itself has allowed us to rapidly collect large amounts of blog data coming from topic categories of interest, by eliminating the need to manually label the data. Table 1 provides a list of the five topic categories used in this study, as well as the total number and the median size of the collected blogs for each. The table also includes the average number of words in each topic category. The blogs were collected in February 2010, starting with the most recent blog posted in each topic and moving back chronologically.

topic category	# of blogs	median size	average # of words
Internet	497	14 kb	986
Cinema and theatre (*sinama va ta'atr*)	255	18 kb	1380
Political (*siyasat-e-rooz*)	500	22 kb	2171
Medical (*pezeshki*)	499	27 kb	2285
Sports (*varzesh*)	498	19 kb	1528

Table 1 – Topic categories of interest and the total number, median size, and average length of the collected blogs for each topic

2.2 Linguistic Parsing

The collected documents are run through a Persian morphological parser that analyzes all word forms including compounds and provides a part of speech tag for the valid analyses [Amtrup 2003]. The morphological analyzer was developed for use in a Persian-English machine translation system and provides part of speech as well as all syntactically relevant inflectional features for a word [cf. Megerdoomian 2000]. The morphological formalism consists of a declarative description of rules utilizing typed feature structures with unification. The morphological analysis component takes advantage of a lexicon of about 40,000 entries in citation form that had been developed in the period of 1999-2002 for coverage of online news articles and includes nouns, adjectives, verbs, adverbs and closed class items. In addition, there are about 5,000 common proper noun entities listed in the lexicon. After morphological analysis, dictionary lookup eliminates all erroneous analyses. Any element that is not successfully associated with a word in the lexicon is tagged as an unknown.

The current morphological analyzer has a coverage of 97% and an accuracy of 93% on a 7MB corpus collected from online news sources. The system fails to analyze conversational forms. Other unanalyzed tokens are mainly proper nouns and words missing in the lexicon.

2.3 Information Gain

To automatically detect the most pertinent unknown terms per blog category, we employ an *information gain* (IG) based feature selection approach. IG's effectiveness as a feature selection measure for text topic categorization, the ultimate objective of this project, has been well studied [Yang and Pedersen 1997].

Information gain is a statistical measure for calculating the expected reduction in *entropy* [Mitchell 1997]. Entropy, a common measure in information theory, captures the impurity of a collection of examples relative to the intended classification. For a binary classification task, the entropy of a set of examples *E* is defined as:

$$Entropy(E) = -p_+ \log_2 p_+ - p_- \log_2 p_-$$

where p_+ is the proportion of positive examples and p_- is the proportion of negative examples in *E*. Moreover, it is assumed that $0 \log_2 0$ is equal to zero. The discriminatory power of an attribute for a given class can then be measured by IG, which is the reduction in entropy caused by the partitioning of the data using that attribute. The IG for example set *E* and attribute *A* is defined as:

$$IG(E, A) = Entropy(E) - \sum_{v \in Values(A)} \frac{|E_v|}{|E|} Entropy(E_v)$$

where *Values*(*A*) represents the set of all possible values that attribute *A* can take on and E_v is the set of examples for which attribute *A* takes on value *v*. In this study, each attribute has a binary value which signifies the presence or absence of a given unknown term in the document. So for the purpos-

[1] www.blogfa.com

es of this study, the above equation can be formulated as:

$$IG(D,t) = Entropy(D) - \frac{|D_t|}{|D|} Entropy(D_t) - \frac{|\overline{D_t}|}{|D|} Entropy(\overline{D_t})$$

where D is the set of all documents, t is a given term, D_t is the set of documents in which term t occurs, and $\overline{D_t}$ is the set of documents in which term t does not occur.

Translit.	Weight	Translation
vyndvz	0.100033	Windows
danlvd	0.080559	download
fayl	0.058319	file
karbran	0.051595	users
Java	0.048287	Java
klyk	0.048180	click
yahv	0.044999	Yahoo
nvkya	0.044807	Nokia
flG	0.042718	Flash
mrvrgr	0.041374	browser
hk	0.041074	hack
msnJr	0.040853	Messenger
Ct	0.039987	chat
psvrd	0.039213	password
kd	0.035936	code

Table 2 –The top weighted unknown terms for the Internet topic category and their associated information gain

Since the aim of feature selection for this paper is that of identifying the most pertinent unknown terms for each topic category, an additional constraint is imposed on the feature selection process. Here, for a term to be selected, it not only needs to have a high IG, but it needs to be present in a higher proportion of positive examples than the negative ones. This prevents the selection of terms that while are good descriptors of the negative class and thus carry a high IG, are not necessarily pertinent to the positive class (i.e., the topic category under consideration). So IG of a term not meeting the above constraint is effectively set to zero.

As indicated previously, the 200 unknown terms with the highest IG for each topic category are thus selected for the analysis portion of this study. Table 2 depicts a sample set of the top weighted terms for the Internet category in transliteration and translation. The transliteration schema was designed to display the results of the morphological analyzer system. It directly represents the Persian script and provides a bijective, one-to-one mapping of the characters. The transliteration omits any diacritics, including vowels, that are not represented in the original script.

2.4 Candidate List

The weight-ordered list of unknown words provides a candidate list of potential neologisms. However, the set of unknown terms extracted from each topic category includes proper names, spelling errors, conversational language forms and neologisms. We therefore manually study the candidate list in order to identify the appropriate classes of neologisms. The results are classified based on the observed linguistic characteristics and a quantitative analysis is performed for each topic category.

3 Neologism Classification

Persian language blogs include a large number of neologisms ranging from new usages in conversational language to newly coined words to designate new technology or political concepts. We performed a qualitative, linguistic investigation of Persian language blogs, consisting of posts from four main categories of technical, political, arts, and personal diary [Megerdoomian 2008]. The goal of this study was to identify elements of Persian Blogspeak that indicate language change and which fail to be analyzed by the existing Persian machine translation and information extraction systems that had been developed for online news sources. The study pointed to four main categories of new word formation found in Persian language blogs:

- Borrowings (mainly from English and French)
- Compounding
- Affixation
- Conversion: Semantic and functional shift

These neologisms were identified based on the prevalent linguistic classification of newly formed words (see for instance the classification of neologisms described in [Grzega and Schoener 2007]).

These four classes of neologisms are described in more detail in the rest of this section.

3.1 Borrowings

A large number of new loan words can be found in blogs. Although they may sometimes be inserted within the text in the original language, they are generally transcribed into Persian script. These loans are used as regular words and can take Persian inflectional affixes. Some examples are provided in Table 3.

Persian	Transcription	Translation
مونیتور	*monitor*	Monitor
فیلترینگشون	*filteringeshun*	their filtering
سایتها	*sâythâ*	sites
پسوردتان	*pasvordetân*	your password
وایرلس	*vâyerles*	Wireless
تایم‌لاین	*tâym lâyn*	Timeline
سکسوالیته	*seksuâliteh*	Sexuality
نوستالژی	*nostâlji*	Nostalgy

Table 3 – Loan words in Persian blogs

An analysis of the occurrence of loans with respect to the various topic domains shows that the Internet category contains a large number of English language loans, whereas the more established scientific domain of medicine tends to use French borrowings. Also within the same category, new technological or scientific additions are generally expressed in English. For instance, in the cinema category, most technical words are of French origin – e.g., اکران from *écran* 'screen' or تیتراژ from *titrage* 'opening credits'. However, new loans have entered the field from English, e.g., انیمیشن *animeyshen* 'animation'.

3.2 Compounding

Compounding is a productive word-formation process in Persian and refers to cases where two or more roots are combined to form a new word. Examples of compounding include راهکار *râhkâr* (consisting of *râh* 'path' and *kâr* 'work' and now being used to mean 'guideline' or 'solution'); سربرگ *sarbarg* (from *sar* 'head' and *barg* 'leaf, piece of paper' signifying 'letterhead'); and دگرباش *degarbâsh* (formed with *degar* 'other' and *bâsh* 'being', meaning 'queer'). In many cases, however, one of the roots is a borrowing that is combined with a Persian root form. Examples of this multilingual compounding construction include تابوسازی *tâbusâzi* (taboo + to make) 'making taboo' and لینکدونی *linkduni* (link + storage) meaning 'blogroll'.

Recently, there has been a concerted effort by the Persian Language Academy to replace borrowings from foreign languages by equivalent Persian constructions. Thus, the traditional هلیکوپتر *helikopter* 'helicopter' has been replaced by بالگرد *bâlgard* by combining Persian *bâl* 'wing' and *gard* 'turn'. Similarly, the French loanword سناریو *senâryo* 'screenplay' is now being replaced by فیلمنامه *filmnâmé* composed of *film* and *nâmé* 'letter, book'.

Persian has a very productive compounding strategy for forming new verbs where a nominal or adjectival root is combined with a light verb, i.e., a verb that has lost some of its semantic value. Many new verbs, especially in the technical domain, are formed following this construction as illustrated in Table 4.

Persian	Transcription	Translation
کلیک کردن	*kelik kardan*	to click
چت کردن	*chat kardan*	to chat
اس‌ام‌اس زدن	*es-em-es zadan*	to send a text message
کنسل شدن	*kansel shodan*	to be cancelled

Table 4 – Compound verb formation

3.3 Affixation

New words are often created following a productive word-formation pattern using suffixes. For instance, the agentive suffix *–gar* is used to form مرورگر *morurgar* 'browser' by combining with *morur* 'review', and فتنه‌گر *fetne-gar* 'seditious' when combined with *fetne* 'sedition'[2]. Another common affix used to form new words is *–estân* which indicates a place. This suffix can be found in terms like وبلاگستان *veblâgestân* (weblog + *-stan*) 'blogosphere' or لینکستان *linkestân* (link + *-stan*) 'blogroll'.

In addition to the compound verb formation, bloggers have started creating simple verbs by combining the verbal ending *–idan* with nominal

[2] *Fetne-gar* is a relatively new creation that is used alongside the traditional *fetne-ju* 'seditious'. There is a clear sense among native speakers, however, that *fetne-gar* refers to a person who is more agentive, actively causing discord.

roots as in چتیدن *chatidan* 'to chat' or لاگیدن *lâgidan* 'to blog'.

3.4 Conversion

Another type of neologism found in Persian language blogs consists of existing words that are being used in a new context, bringing about a semantic shift. In certain instances, the part-of-speech category may also shift. One example is the adjective شفاف *shafâf* 'transparent' that is being used more and more frequently as an adverb in political contexts with the meaning 'openly, transparently'.

This category, however, is difficult to detect automatically with the methodology used since these words already exist in traditional lexicons and are not tagged as unknowns by the morphological parser. Identifying conversions and semantic shifts currently requires a manual exploration of the data; we leave a study of this class of neologisms for future work.

4 Topic and Neologism Correspondence

An investigation of the neologisms for each topic category clearly suggests that there is a close relationship between the class of neologisms and the topic domain.

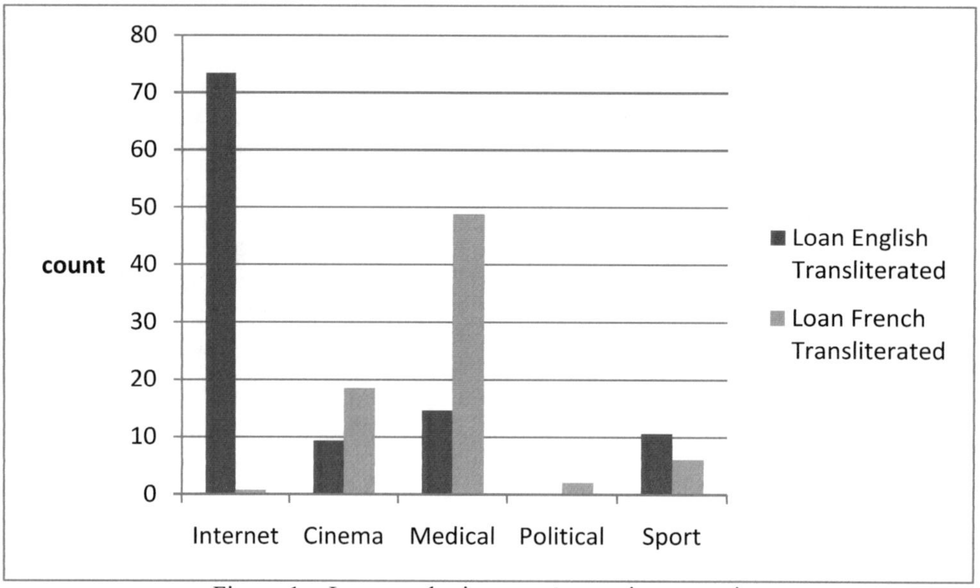

Figure 1 – Loan neologisms across topic categories

Starting from the weight-ordered candidate list for each topic category, we manually examined and labeled each unknown word according to the neologism classification described in Section 3. In order to identify the correct class, each unknown word was considered within its context of occurrence in the corresponding blog posts and classified according to the usage within the sentence. In addition, proper names, conversational forms of existing words, and spelling errors were tagged separately.

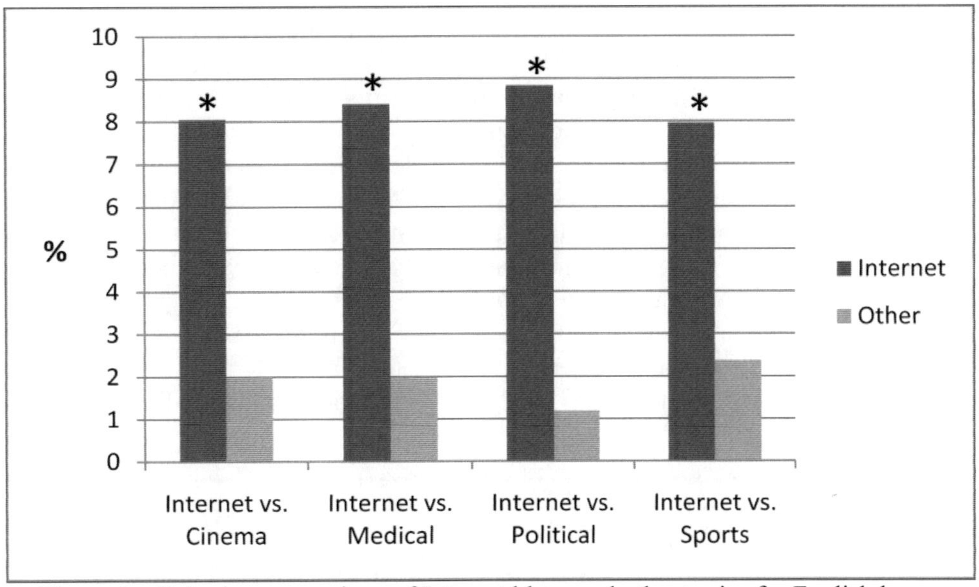

Figure 2 – Pairwise comparison of Internet blogs and other topics for English loans

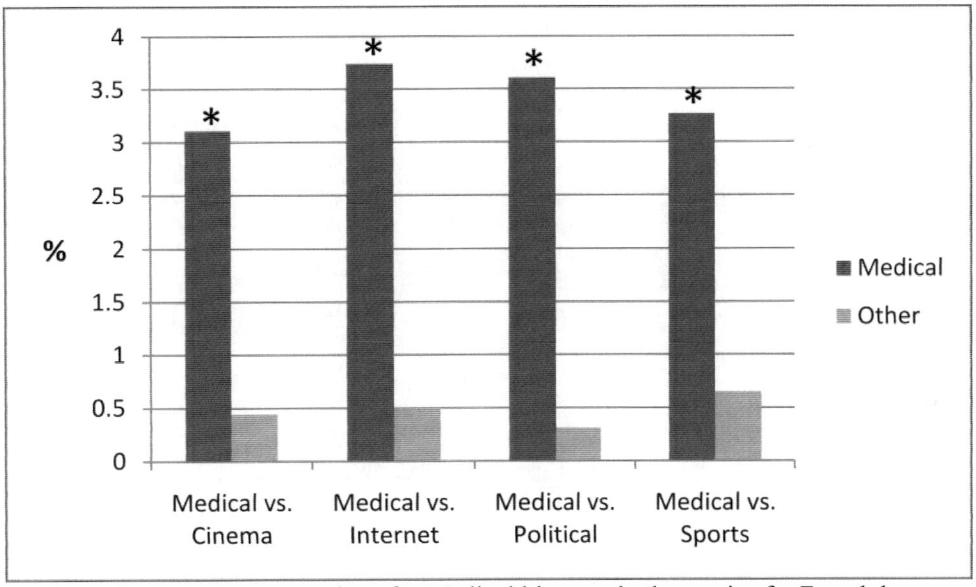

Figure 3 – Pairwise comparison for Medical blogs and other topics for French loans

Figure 1 illustrates the correspondence of the number of borrowings per topic category in the corresponding candidate list. The results show that the most common way of forming new words within blogs dealing with Internet and computer technology is to use borrowings from English. In the medical domain, however, most neologisms are scientific terms borrowed mainly from the French language. The domain of cinema and theatre also includes a large number of loans from French. However, most of the French loans across topics seem to be older borrowings while the newer loans (i.e, within the last three to five years) are almost always from the English language. A statistical analysis of the results indicate that these correspondences are significant as shown in Figure 2 for English loans and in Figure 3 for French loans. Figure 2 illustrates a pairwise comparison between the Internet category and other blog topics based on the average percentage of documents in which a given term from the English loan neologism category is included. (*) indicates a statistically significant difference between the two percentages. Figure 3 shows a similar result for the pairwise comparison between the Medical category and other topics for the French loan class.

Figure 4 shows the relative usage of affixation and compounding strategies for the creation of new words. Although affixation is used to some degree in both the Internet and medical domains, they do not occur as often as the English or French loans (cf. Figure 1 above). Interestingly, the blogs that fall within the political topic category do not make much use of borrowings from English and French. Instead, they tend to create new words by applying productive affixation and compounding strategies. In most instances, the words used to form neologisms in the politics category are based on words of Arabic and Persian origin. Figure 5 illustrates the pairwise comparison between the Political and other blog topics based on the average percentage of documents in which a given term from the affixation and compounding class of neologisms is included. (*) indicates a statistically significant difference between the two percentages.

Hence, while the Internet blogs make heavy use of English loans in the creation of new words, political blogs tend to use affixation and compound strategies for word-formation. These results sug-

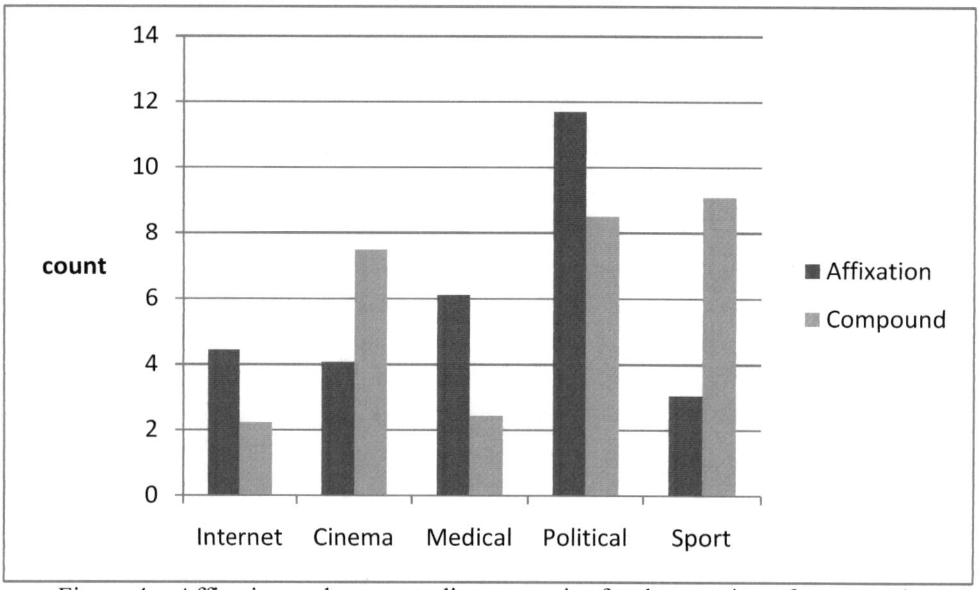

Figure 4 – Affixation and compounding strategies for the creation of new words across various blog topics

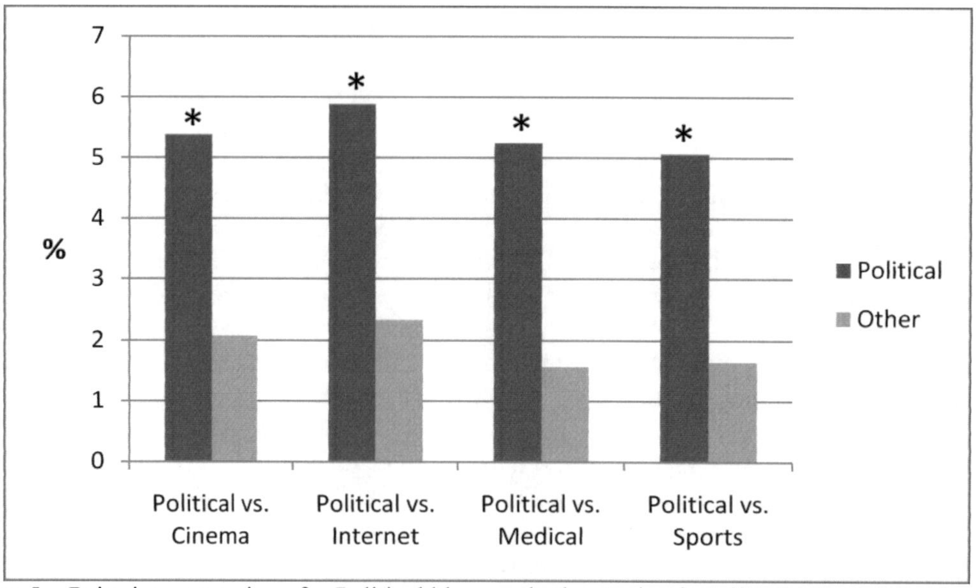

Figure 5 – Pairwise comparison for Political blogs and other topics for affixation and compounding

gest that, depending on the domain of interest for the particular NLP application, distinct methodologies for the automatic detection and processing of neologisms should be implemented.

5 Conclusion

This paper presents an investigation of neologisms in Persian blog posts across five distinct topic areas. We employ morphological analysis in conjunction with a profile-based classification technique to successfully extract a pertinent candidate list for identifying new word-level constructions in blogs. These neologisms are then classified based on their linguistic characteristics and word-formation strategies and the quantitative analysis points to a significant correspondence between neologism classes and blog topic domains.

Based on these results, we propose that the detection and processing strategies should be tailored to the domain of the NLP application for greater efficiency. In particular, a derivational morphological system can be developed by implementing the productive affixation and compounding rules used in Persian word formation. This system can be used to extend the existing analysis and translation systems in the domain of politics. Loans from English, on the other hand, can be automatically processed by using previously implemented methodologies for transcribing Persian script into the English writing system [Megerdoomian 2006, Johanson 2007]. Such a system would be beneficial in recognizing the large number of loans encountered in the technical and scientific domains.

This work is part of a larger project for automatic topic classification and sentiment analysis in Persian language blogs. We extract the most pertinent neologisms encountered in the blog corpus in order to enhance the topic classification system. In addition, the results obtained will be used to extend the current morphological parser to improve coverage and identification of newly formed words.

References

Amtrup, Jan W. 2003. Morphology in machine translation systems: Efficient integration of finite state transducers and feature structure descriptions. *Machine Translation,* 18(3), pp. 217-238.

Grzega, Joachim and Marion Schoener. 2007. *English and general historical lexicology: Materials for onomasiology seminars.* Onomasiology Online Monographs, Vol. 1. Germany.

Ittner, D.J., Lewis, D.D., and Ahn, D.D. (1995). Text categorization of low quality images. In Symposium on Document Analysis and Information Retrieval. Las Vegas, NV.

Johanson, Joshua. 2007. Transcription of names written in Farsi into English. In *Proceedings of the Computational Approaches to Arabic Script-based Languages* (CAASL2). LSA Linguistic Institute, Stanford.

Kelly, John and Bruce Etling (2008). Mapping Iran's online public: Politics and culture in the Persian blogosphere. Research Publication No. 2008-01, The Berkman Center for Internet and Society at Harvard Law School. April 6.

Megerdoomian, Karine. 2008. Analysis of Farsi weblogs. MITRE Tech Report 080206. August 2008.

Megerdoomian, Karine. 2006. Transcription of Persian proper name entities into English. Technical report, Inxight Software, Inc.

Megerdoomian, Karine. 2000. Unification-based Persian morphology. In *Proceedings of CICLing 2000.* Alexander Gelbukh, ed. Centro de Investigacion en Computacion-IPN, Mexico.

Mitchell, Tom M. 1997. *Machine learning*. McGraw-Hill.

Pacea, Otilia. 2009. New worlds, new words: On language change and word formation in Internet English and Romanian. In *The annals of Ovidius University Constanta- Philology*, issue 20, pp: 87-102.

Salton, G. 1991. Developments in automatic text retrieval. Science, v.253: 974-980.

Sebastiani, F. 2002. Machine learning in automated text categorization. In ACM Computing Surveys, 34(1): 1-47

Sifry, Dave. 2007. The Technorati state of the live web: April 2007.

Yang, Yiming and Jan Pedersen, J.O. 1997. A comparative study on feature selection in text categorization. In *Proceedings of International Conference on Machine Learning.*

Comparing Semantic Role Labeling with Typed Dependency Parsing in Computational Metaphor Identification

Eric P. S. Baumer
Department of Informatics
Univ of California, Irvine
5029 Donald Bren Hall
Irvine, CA 92627-3440 USA
ebaumer@ics.uci.edu

James P. White
School of Information and Computer Sciences
Univ of California, Irvine
Irvine, CA 92627
jpwhite@uci.edu

Bill Tomlinson
Department of Informatics
Univ of California, Irvine
5068 Donald Bren Hall
Irvine, CA 92627-3440 USA
wmt@uci.edu

Abstract

Most computational approaches to metaphor have focused on discerning between metaphorical and literal text. Recent work on computational metaphor identification (CMI) instead seeks to identify overarching conceptual metaphors by mapping selectional preferences between source and target corpora. This paper explores using semantic role labeling (SRL) in CMI. Its goals are two-fold: first, to demonstrate that semantic roles can effectively be used to identify conceptual metaphors, and second, to compare SRL to the current use of typed dependency parsing in CMI. The results show that SRL can be used to identify potential metaphors and that it overcomes some of the limitations of using typed dependencies, but also that SRL introduces its own set of complications. The paper concludes by suggesting future directions, both for evaluating the use of SRL in CMI, and for fostering critical and creative thinking about metaphors.

1 Introduction

Metaphor, the partial framing of one concept in terms of another, pervades human language and thought (Lakoff and Johnson, 1980; Lakoff, 1993). A variety of computational approaches to metaphorical language have been developed, e.g., (Martin, 1990; Fass, 1991; Gedigian et al., 2006; Krishnakumaran and Zhu, 2007). However, most such methods see metaphor as an obstacle to be overcome in the task of discerning the actual, literal meaning of a phrase or sentence.

In contrast, the work presented here approaches conceptual metaphor not as an obstacle but as a resource. Metaphor is an integral part in human understanding of myriad abstract or complex concepts (Lakoff and Johnson, 1980), and metaphorical thinking can be a powerful component in critical and creative thinking, cf. (Gordon, 1974; Oxman-Michelli, 1991). However, "because they can be used so automatically and effortlessly, we find it hard to question [metaphors], if we can even notice them" (Lakoff and Turner, 1989, p. 65). Computational metaphor identification (CMI) (Baumer, 2009; Baumer et al., under review) addresses this difficulty by identifying potential conceptual metaphors in written text. Rather than attempting to discern whether individual phrases are metaphorical or literal, this technique instead identifies larger, overarching linguistic patterns. The goal of CMI is not to state definitively *the* metaphor present in a text, but rather to draw potential metaphors to readers' attention, thereby encouraging both critical examination of current metaphors and creative generation of alternative metaphors.

CMI identifies potential metaphors by mapping selectional preferences (Resnik, 1993) from a source corpus to a target corpus. Previous work on CMI utilized typed dependency parses (de Marneffe et al., 2006) to calculate these selectional preferences. This paper explores the use of semantic role labeling (SRL) (Gildea and Jurafsky, 2002; Johansson and Nugues, 2008) to calculate selectional preferences. Typed dependencies focus on syntactic structure and grammatical relations, while semantic roles emphasize conceptual and semantic structure, so SRL may

Proceedings of the NAACL HLT 2010 Second Workshop on Computational Approaches to Linguistic Creativity, pages 14–22,
Los Angeles, California, June 2010. ©2010 Association for Computational Linguistics

be more effective for identifying potential conceptual metaphors. This paper describes how SRL was incorporated into CMI and compares both the relational data and the metaphors identified with typed dependency parsing and semantic role labeling. The results show that semantic roles enabled effective identification of potential metaphors. However, neither typed dependencies nor semantic roles were necessarily superior. Rather, each provides certain advantages, both in terms of identifying potential metaphors, and in terms of promoting critical thinking and creativity.

2 Related Work

2.1 Computational Approaches to Metaphor

Many computational approaches have been taken toward identifying metaphor in written text. MIDAS (Martin, 1990) attempts to detect when users of the Unix Consultant command line help system use metaphors, for example, "How do I enter Emacs?" is interpreted as "How do I invoke Emacs?" Another system, met* (Fass, 1991), is designed to distinguish both metaphor and metonymy from literal text, providing special techniques for processing these instances of figurative language. More recently, Gedigian et al. (2006) used hand-annotated corpora to train an automatic metaphor classifier. Krishnakumaran and Zhu (2007) used violations of WordNet-based (Fellbaum, 1998) verb-noun expectations to identify the presence of a metaphor, e.g., "he is a brave lion," would be considered metaphorical, because "he," taken to mean a "person," which is not a WordNet hyponym of "lion."

These and similar approaches ascribe to some degree to the literal meaning hypothesis (Reddy, 1969), which states that every sentence has a literal meaning, as derived from the meanings of its constituent words, while some also have a figurative meaning that goes beyond the meanings of the words themselves. In this view, a figurative interpretation is only sought only after a literal interpretation has been formed and found inconsistent, nonsensical, or otherwise faulty. However, experimental evidence has made this account suspect (Gibbs, 1984; Gentner et al., 2001). Even distinguishing whether a given expression is literal or figurative can be difficult at best. For example, "the rock is becoming brittle with age" (Reddy, 1969, p. 242), has "a literal interpretation when uttered about a stone and a metaphorical one when said about a decrepit professor emeritus" (Fass, 1991, p. 54).

One previous metaphor system avoids making such literal/metaphorical distinctions. CorMet (Mason, 2004) is designed to extract known conventional metaphors from domain-specific textual corpora, which are derived from Google queries. CorMet calculates selectional preferences and associations (Resnik, 1993) for each corpus's characteristic verbs, i.e., those verbs at least twice as frequent in the corpus as in general English. Based on these selectional associations, CorMet clusters the nouns for which the characteristic verbs select. To identify metaphors, mappings are sought from clusters in the source corpus to clusters in the target corpus, based on the degree to which the same verbs select for members of both clusters. For example, CorMet was used to extract the metaphor MONEY IS A LIQUID[1] by mapping from a cluster for the concept *liquid* in a corpus for the domain LABORATORY to a cluster for the concept *money* in a corpus for the domain FINANCE, based on the selectional associations of verbs such as "pour," "flow," "freeze," and "evaporate." The CMI system described in this paper is informed largely by CorMet (Mason, 2004).

2.2 Semantic Role Labeling

While interpretations vary somewhat, semantic role labeling (SRL) generally aims to represent something about the meaning of a phrase at a deeper level than surface syntactic structure. One of the most common approaches to performing SRL automatically is to use a statistical classifier trained on labeled corpora (Gildea and Jurafsky, 2002), with FrameNet (Baker et al., 1998) and PropBank (Palmer et al., 2005) being the primary sources. An important result of the Gildea and Jurafsky work was identifying the significant utility of using presegmented constituents as input to their labeler, and accordingly most SRL systems perform a syntactic analysis as an initial step.

The principal alternative to using a statistical classifier is to use a rule-based labeler for operating on

[1] SMALL CAPS are metaphors, *italics* are concepts, CAPS are domains, and "quotes" are example phrases.

the syntactic parse tree. For example, Shi and Mihalcea (2004) extract explicit SRL rules by analyzing FrameNet cases. Another system, RelEx (Fundel et al., 2006) also uses rules and is structured like the implementation used here (see below for details), but despite having the same name, is a different system. Statistical and rule-based methods may also be used within the same system, such as in LTH (Johansson and Nugues, 2008).

One reason for preferring a rule-based SRL system is that rule-based approaches may be less susceptible to the loss of accuracy that statistically trained classifiers suffer when applied to domains that are different than the corpora they are trained on (Johansson and Nugues, 2008). That problem is compounded by the limited domain coverage provided by the labeled corpora currently available for SRL classifier training (Gildea and Jurafsky, 2002).

3 Computational Metaphor Identification

While space precludes a fully detailed description of the algorithms involved, this section provides a high-level summary of the techniques employed in CMI (Baumer, 2009; Baumer et al., under review).

Metaphors are conceptual mappings wherein a source concept partially structures the understanding of a target concept. In ELECTION IS WAR, the target concept *election* is partially framed in terms of the source concept *war*. CMI begins by gathering corpora for the source and target domains. In this paper, the target corpus consists of posts from political blogs, described in more detail in the methods section below. Source corpora are composed of Wikipedia articles, as they provide a readily available, categorically organized, large source of content on a wide variety of topics. A source corpus for a given domain consists of all the Wikipedia articles in the category for that domain, as well as all articles in its subcategories. All documents in the source and target corpora are parsed to extract sentence structure and typed dependencies (Klein and Manning, 2003; de Marneffe et al., 2006).

The crux of CMI is selectional preference learning (Resnik, 1993), which quantifies the tendency of particular words to appear with certain other classes of words in specific grammatical relationships. For example, words for the concept of food are often the direct object of the verb "eat." Using the parsed documents, CMI calculates selectional preferences of the characteristic nouns in a corpus, where characteristic means that the noun is highly frequent in the corpus relative to its frequency in general English, as derived from (Kilgarriff, 1996). Selectional preference is quantified as the relative entropy of the posterior distribution conditioned on a specific noun and grammatical relation with respect to the prior distribution of verbs in general English:

$$S(c) = \sum_{v} P(v|c) \log \frac{P(v|c)}{P(v)} \qquad (1)$$

where c is a class of nouns (i.e., a concept like food) and a grammatical relation (such as direct object), and v ranges over all the verbs for which c appears in the given relation. These selectional preference strengths are then divided among the verbs that appear in each grammatical relation to determine the noun class's selectional association for each verb in each relation (Resnik, 1993).

Selectional associations are calculated for classes of words, but the corpora consist of words that may represent many possible classes of nouns. Thus, individual nouns count as partial observations of each word class that they might represent using WordNet (Fellbaum, 1998). For example, "vote," "primary," and "runoff" can all represent the concept of *election*. Here we use a customized version of WordNet that includes major political figures from the 2008 US Election. These word classes are then clustered using two-nearest-neighbor clustering based on the verbs for which they select. Each cluster represents a coherent concept in the corpus, and each is automatically labeled based on the synsets it contains.

This approach of using clustered hypernyms resonates with Lakoff's argument that metaphorical mappings occur not at the level of situational specifics, but at the superordinate level. For example, in the metaphor LOVE IS A JOURNEY, the relationship is a vehicle. Although specific instantiations of the metaphor may frame that vehicle variously as a train ("off the track"), a car ("long, bumpy road"), or a plane ("just taking off"), "the categories mapped will tend to be at the superordinate level rather than the basic level" (Lakoff, 1993, p. 212). This method of counting each word observed as a partial observation of each of the synsets it might represent causes observations at the basic level to accumulate in the superordinate levels they collectively represent. This is not to say that hierarchical conceptual relations capture every possible metaphor, but rather that these are the relations on which we focus here.

To identify metaphors, CMI looks for correspondences between conceptual clusters in the source and target corpora. For example, in the Military corpus, the cluster for *war* would frequently select to be the direct object of "win," the object of the preposition "during" with the verb "fight," the object of the preposition "in" with the verb "defeated," and so on. In some blog corpora, the cluster for *election* also selects for those same verbs in the same grammatical relationships. Based on the similarity of these selectional associations, each mapping is given a confidence score to indicate how likely the linguistic patterns are to evidence a conceptual metaphor. One of the strengths of CMI is that it works in the aggregate. While individual instances of phrases such as "fought during the election" and "defeated in the primary" may not at first glance appear metaphorical, it is the systematicity of these patterns that becomes compelling evidence for the existence of a metaphor.

An important aspect of CMI is that it identifies only linguistic patterns potentially indicative of conceptual metaphors, not the metaphors themselves. As mentioned above, Lakoff (1993) emphasizes that metaphor is primarily a cognitive phenomenon, and that metaphorical language serves as evidence for the cognitive phenomenon. CMI leverages computational power to search through large bodies of text to identify patterns of potential interest, then presents those patterns to a human user along with the potential metaphors they might imply to foster critical thinking about metaphor. To reiterate, this places the job of finding patterns in the hands of the computer, and the job of interpreting those patterns in the hands of the human user.

4 CMI with Semantic Role Labeling

The work presented in this paper attempts to enhance CMI by using SRL to expand the types of relations between nouns and verbs that can be seen as instantiating a metaphor. The prior CMI implementation treats each grammatical dependency type as a distinct relation. For example, in the sentence, "The city contained a sacred grove for performing religious rites," "rites" is the direct object of "perform," as denoted by the *dobj* dependency. However, the sentence, "The religious rites were once again performed openly," uses a passive construction, meaning that "rites" is the passive subject, or *nsubjpass*, of "perform." With SRL, the relations between "perform" and "rite" are the same for both sentences; specifically, *Intentionally_act:Act* ("rite" is the intentional act being performed) and *Transitive_action:Patient* ("rite" is the recipient of a transitive action). Because the relations in FrameNet are organized into an inheritance structure, both the more general frame *Transitive_action* and the more specialized frame *Intentionally_act* apply here.

This section describes how SRL was incorporated into CMI, compares the component data derived from SRL with the data derived from a typed dependency parse, and compares resulting identified metaphors.

4.1 Implementation Methods

The CMI system used here takes the prior implementation (described in section 3) and replaces the Stanford typed dependency parser (de Marneffe et al., 2006) with the RelEx SRL system (http://opencog.org/wiki/RelEx). RelEx performs a full syntactic parse, then applies a set of syntactic pattern rules to annotate the parse tree with role labels based (not exactly or completely) on FrameNet. This implementation uses a rule-based labeler because CMI hinges on differences in selectional preferences in corpora from different domains, and statistically trained classifiers are biased by the distributions of the corpora on which they are trained.

For syntactic parsing, RelEx uses the Link Grammar Parser (LGP) which is based on the Link Grammar model (Sleator and Temperley, 1993). LGP produces output very similar to typed dependencies. The version of RelEx we use integrates the Another Nearly-New Information Extraction (ANNIE) system (http://gate.ac.uk/sale/tao/splitch6.html#chap:annie) to tag named entities. Sentences are split using the OpenNLP sentence splitter (http://opennlp.sourceforge.net/).

Because CMI's corpora are acquired from public

	Blogs	Religion (Wikipedia)
Docs	546 (604)	3289 (3294)
Sents	5732 (6708)	128,543 (145,193)
Words	148,619	3,300,455

Table 1: Sizes of the target and source corpora; parentheses show totals including documents without valid sentences and sentences with no relations.

Internet sources, the text must be cleaned to make it suitable for parsing. Text from Wikipedia articles undergoes many small filtering steps in order to remove wiki markup, omit article sections that do not consist primarily of prose (e.g., "See Also" and "References"), and decompose Unicode letters and punctuation into compatibility form. Wikipedia articles also tend to use bulleted lists in the middle of sentences rather than comma-separated clauses. We attempt to convert those constructions back into sentences, which only sometimes results in a reasonable sentence. However, it helps to ensure that the following sentence is properly recognized by the sentence splitter. For blog posts, HTML tags were removed, which at times required multiple decoding passes due to improperly configured blog feeds, and characters decomposed into compatible form.

4.2 Data

Table 1 shows statistics on the sizes of the source and target corpora. Numbers in parentheses are totals, including blank documents and sentences with no valid relations. There are some sentences for which RelEx does not produce any parse, e.g., long sentences that LGP deems ungrammatical. The Stanford parser produced some result for every sentence, because it will produce a result tree for any kind of text, even if it does not recognize any grammatically valid tokens.

Table 2 lists the number of verb-noun relations for each corpus, with parentheses showing average relations per word. Since RelEx often labels the same verb-noun relation with multiple hierarchically-related frames (as described above), Table 2 also lists the number of unique verb-noun pairs labeled. For the blogs corpus, the Stanford parser generated 111 distinct dependency types, while RelEx labeled 1446 distinct roles. The ten

Stanford	Blogs	Religion
Reln(v, n)	19,303 (2.88)	425,367 (2.93)
Unique(v, n)	19,303 (2.88)	425,367 (2.93)
RelEx	Blogs	Religion
Reln(v, n)	57,639 (8.59)	1,219,345 (8.40)
Unique(v, n)	20,962 (3.12)	482,997 (3.33)

Table 2: Relations for the target and source corpora; parentheses show average relations per word.

Stanford		RelEx	
Relation	Freq	Relation	Freq
dobj	3815	Transitive_action:Patient	4268
nsubj	3739	Transitive_action:Agent	3597
prep_in	1072	Inheritance:Item_2	1489
prep_to	695	Categorization:Category	1489
prep_on	563	Attributes:Attribute	1488
nsubjpass	528	Existence:Entity	1277
prep_for	491	Categorization:Item	1270
prep_with	435	Inheritance:Item_1	1269
prep_at	285	Attributes:Entity	1268
dep	279	Purpose:Means	569

Table 3: Most common dependencies and frequencies.

most common of each are listed with their frequencies in Table 3.

These data show that RelEx provides more information, both in terms of successfully parsing more sentences, and in terms of relations-per-word. The next section explores the impact of these differences on identified metaphors.

4.3 Results

This section describes metaphors identified when mapping from the RELIGION source corpus to the political blogs target corpus. CMI results are usually culled to include only the upper one percentile in terms of confidence, but space constraints prohibit a full analysis of even this upper one percentile. Instead, this section compares mappings with the highest confidence score from the typed dependency data and from the semantic role data. RELIGION was chosen as the source domain because the highest confidence metaphors from both typed dependencies and semantic roles had similar target and source concepts, facilitating a better comparison. This analysis

Target (label and cluster)	Source (label and cluster)	Conf
medicine - {medicine, medical specialty}, {medicine, medication, medicament, medicinal drug}, {music, medicine}, {medicine, practice of medicine}, {learned profession}, {drug}, {social control}, {profession}, {punishment, penalty, penalization, penalisation}, {life science, bioscience}	**sacrament** - {sacrament}, {baptism}, {religious ceremony, religious ritual}	1.968
	ritual - {ceremony}, {practice, pattern}, {custom, usage, usance}, {ritual, rite}, {survival}	1.465

Table 4: Metaphors for *medicine* from RELIGION using typed dependencies.

is not intended to demonstrate that either technique is superior (for more on possible evaluation methods, see Discussion section below). Rather, it provides a detailed depiction of both to ascertain potential benefits and drawbacks of each.

Table 4 presents the strongest two mappings from RELIGION: MEDICINE IS A SACRAMENT and MEDICINE IS A RITUAL; these were the only mappings for *medicine* in the upper one percentile. Each mapping lists both the automatically identified labels and the full cluster contents for source and target, along with the confidence score. The table can be read left-to-right, e.g., "medicine is like a sacrament." Confidence scores typically fall in the range (0, 5) with a few high-confidence mappings and many low-confidence mappings; see (Baumer, 2009; Baumer et al., under review) for details of confidence score calculation. Table 5 shows details for each mapping, including the verb-relation pairs that mediate the mapping, along with an example fragment from the target and source corpora for each verb-relation. These examples show why and how medicine might be like, variously, a sacrament or a ritual; both are "practiced," "administered," "performed," etc. Note that the passive subject and direct object relations are treated as distinct, e.g., "Eucharist is variously administered" involves a different grammatical relation than "administer the sacrament," even though the word for *sacrament* plays a similar semantic role in both fragments.

Tables 6 and 7 show mappings resulting from semantic roles labeled by RelEx, with formats similar to those of tables 4 and 5, except that the verb-relations in table 7 are semantic roles rather than grammatical relations. The mapping in table 6 was the strongest mapping from RELIGION and the only mapping for *medication*.

Table 7 shows how RelEx can treat different grammatical relations as the same semantic role. For example, "medicine is practiced" and "practice the rites" use passive subjective and direct object, respectively, but are both treated as the patient of a transitive action. Such examples confirm that SRL is, at least to some extent, performing the job for which it was intended.

However, these results also expose some problems with SRL, or at least with RelEx's implementation thereof. For example, the phrase "dispose of prescription drugs" is labeled with four separate semantic roles, which is an instance of a single verb-noun relation being labeled with both a superordinate relation, *Physical_entity:Entity*, and a subordinate relation, *Physical_entity:Constituents* (the constituents of a physical entity are themselves an entity). While various approaches might avoid multiple labels, e.g., using only the most general or most specific frame, those are beyond the scope here.

5 Discussion

As mentioned above, these results do not provide conclusive evidence that either typed dependencies or semantic roles are more effective for identifying potential metaphors. However, they do provide an understanding of both techniques' strengths and weaknesses for this purpose, and they also suggest ways in which each may be more or less effective at fostering critical and creative thinking.

For metaphor identification, the previous section described how typed dependency parsing treats passive subjects and direct object as distinct relations, whereas SRL will at times conflate them into identical patient roles. This means that the typed dependency-based metaphors appear to be mediated by a greater number of relations. However, it also

Target	Source	Verb-Reln	Target Ex Frag	Source Ex Frag
medicine	sacrament	practice - nsubjpass	"**medicine** is **practiced**"	"**rites** were **practiced**"
		administer - nsubjpass	"**antibiotics** are regularly **administered**"	"**Eucharist** is variously **administered**"
		administer - dobj	"**administered medicines**"	"**administer** the **sacrament**"
		perform - dobj	"**perform** defensive **medicine**"	"**performed** the last **rites**"
		receive - dobj	"**received** conventional **medicines**"	"**received** the **rites**"
	ritual	perform - dobj	"**perform** defensive **medicine**"	"**performed** the last **rites**"
		practice - nsubjpass	"**medicine** is **practiced**"	"**ceremonies** are also **practiced**"
		administer - dobj	"**administered medicines**"	"**administering** the **rites**"
		administer - nsubjpass	"**antibiotics** are regularly **administered**"	"**sacrament** is ordinarily **administered**"

Table 5: Details of RELIGION metaphors from typed dependencies, including mediators and example phrases.

Target (label and cluster)	Source (label and cluster)	Conf
medication - {medicine, medication, medicament, medicinal drug}, {drug}, {agent}	**ceremony** - {ceremony}, {sacrament}, {rite, religious rite}, {religious ceremony, religious ritual}	2.570

Table 6: Metaphor for *medication* from RELIGION using semantic roles.

Target	Source	Verb-Reln	Target Ex Frag	Source Ex Frag
medication	ceremony	practice - Transitive_action:Patient	"**medicine** is **practiced**"	"**practice** the **rites**"
		perform - Transitive_action:Patient	"**perform** defensive **medicine**"	"**perform** most religious **rites**"
		include - Transitive_action:Agent	"**medicine including**"	"**liturgies included**"
		dispose - Physical_entity:Constituents	"**dispose** of prescription **drugs**"	"**disposed** of without **ceremony**"
		dispose - Inheritance:Instance	"**dispose** of prescription **drugs**"	"**disposed** of without **ceremony**"
		dispose - Inheritance:Group	"**dispose** of prescription **drugs**"	"**disposed** of without **ceremony**"
		dispose - Physical_entity:Entity	"**dispose** of prescription **drugs**"	"**disposed** of without **ceremony**"

Table 7: Details of RELIGION metaphors from semantic roles, including mediators and example phrases.

means that less data are available to the selection preference calculation, in that there are fewer observations for each relation. On the other hand, SRL is a much finer-grained classification than typed dependencies. The implementation used here included 111 grammatical relations, whereas RelEx labeled 1446 distinct roles. Thus, overall, RelEx may be providing fewer observations for each relation, but those relations may have more semantic import.

For fostering critical thinking and creativity, a key concern is making identified metaphors readily comprehensible. Ortony (Ortony, 1980) and others have suggested that selectional restriction violations are an important component of metaphor comprehension. Therefore, tools that employ CMI often present parallel source and target fragments side-by-side to make clear the selectional restriction violation, e.g., metaViz, a system for presenting computationally identified metaphors in political blogs (Baumer et al., 2010). One might assume that typed dependencies are more readily comprehensible, since they are expressed as relatively simple grammatical relations. However, when presenting example fragments to users, there is no need to explicate the nature of the relationship being demonstrated, but rather the parallel examples can simply be placed side-by-side. It is an empirical question whether users would see phrases such as "medicine is practiced" and "practice the rites" as parallel examples of the same psycholinguistic relationship. Thus, the question of whether typed dependencies or semantic roles better facilitate metaphor comprehension may not be as important as the question of whether example phrases are perceived as parallel.

6 Future Work

This paper is only an initial exploration, demonstrating that semantic role labeling is viable for use in CMI. For the sake of comparison, the analysis here focuses on examples where metaphors identified using the two techniques were relatively similar. However, such similarity does not always occur. For example, using MILITARY as the source domain, typed dependencies led to results such as A NOMINEE IS A FORCE and A NOMINEE IS AN ARMY, whereas semantic roles gave mappings including AN INDIVIDUAL IS A WEAPON (here, the label "individual" is a superordinate category including mostly politicians), and THE US IS A SOLDIER. Future work should analyze these differences in more detail to provide a broad and deep comparison across multiple source domains and target corpora.

But how should such an analysis be conducted? That is, how does one determine which identified metaphors are "better," and by what standard? In suggesting a number of potential evaluation methods for CMI, Baumer et al. (under review) argue that the most sensible approach is asking human subjects to assess metaphors, potentially along a variety of criteria. For example: Does the metaphor make sense? Is it unexpected? Is it confusing? Such assessments could help evaluate semantic roles vs. typed dependencies in two ways. First, does either parsing technique lead to metaphors that are consistently assessed by subjects as better? Second, does either parsing technique lead to better alignment (i.e., stronger correlations) between human assessments and CMI confidence scores? Such subjective assessments could provide evidence for an argument that either typed dependencies or semantic roles are more effective at identifying conceptual metaphors.

7 Conclusion

This paper explores using semantic role labeling (SRL) as a technique for improving computational metaphor identification (CMI). The results show that SRL can be successfully incorporated into CMI. Furthermore, they suggest that SRL may be more effective at identifying relationships with semantic import than typed dependency parsing, but that SRL may also make distinctions that are too fine-grained to serve as effective input for the selectional preference learning involved in CMI. The results also demonstrate that, even though the notion of semantic roles may seem more complex than typed dependencies from a user's perspective, it is possible to present either in a way that may be readily comprehensible. Thus, while more work is necessary to compare these two parsing techniques more fully, semantic role labeling may present an effective means of improving CMI, both in terms of the technical process of identifying conceptual metaphors, and in terms of the broader goal of fostering critical thinking and creativity.

Acknowledgments

This material is based on work supported by the National Science Foundation under Grant No. IIS-0757646, by the Donald Bren School of Information and Computer Sciences, by the California Institute for Telecommunications and Information Technology (Calit2), and by the Undergraduate Research Opportunities Program (UROP) at UCI.

References

Colin F. Baker, Charles J. Fillmore, and John B. Lowe. 1998. The Berkeley FrameNet project. In *Proc 17th Int'l Conf on Comp Ling*, pages 86–90, Montral, Quebec, Canada.

Eric P. S. Baumer, Jordan Sinclair, and Bill Tomlinson. 2010. "America is like Metamucil:" Critical and creative thinking about metaphor in political blogs. In *ACM SIGCHI Conf*, Atlanta, GA. ACM Press.

Eric P. S. Baumer, David Hubin, and Bill Tomlinson. under review. Computational metaphor identification.

Eric Baumer. 2009. *Computational Metaphor Identification to Foster Critical Thinking and Creativity*. Dissertation, University of California, Irvine, Department of Informatics.

Marie-Catherine de Marneffe, Bill MacCartney, and Christopher D. Manning. 2006. Generating typed dependency parses from phrase structure parses. In *Lang Res and Eval (LREC)*, Genoa, Italy.

Dan Fass. 1991. Met*: A method for discriminating metonymy and metaphor by computer. *Comp Ling*, 17(1):49–90.

Christine Fellbaum. 1998. *WordNet: An Electronic Lexical Database*. MIT Press, Cambridge, MA.

Katrin Fundel, Robert Kuffner, and Ralf Zimmer. 2006. RelEx-Relation extraction using dependency parse trees. *Bioinformatics*, 23(3):365–371.

Matt Gedigian, John Bryant, Srini Narayanan, and Branimir Ciric. 2006. Catching metaphors. In *3rd Workshop on Scalable Natural Language Understanding*, New York City. Assoc Comp Ling.

Dedre Gentner, Brian F. Bowdle, Phillip Wolff, and C. Boronat. 2001. Metaphor is like analogy. In Dedre Gentner, Keith J. Holyoak, and Boicho Kokinov, editors, *The Analogical Mind*, pages 199–253. MIT Press, Cambridge, MA.

Raymond W. Gibbs. 1984. Literal meaning and psychological theory. *Cognitive Science*, 8:275–304.

Daniel Gildea and Daniel Jurafsky. 2002. Automatic labeling of semantic roles. *Comp Ling*, 28(3):245–288.

W.J.J. Gordon. 1974. Some source material in discovery-by-analogy. *Journal of Creative Behavior*, 8:239–257.

Richard Johansson and Pierre Nugues. 2008. Dependency-based semantic role labeling of PropBank. In *Proc Conf on Empirical Meth in Nat Lang Proc*, pages 69–78, Honolulu, HI. Assoc Comp Ling.

Adam Kilgarriff. 1996. BNC word frequency list. http://www.kilgarriff.co.uk/bnc-readme.html.

Dan Klein and Christopher D. Manning. 2003. Accurate unlexicalized parsing. In *Mtg of the Assoc for Comp Ling*, Sapporo, Japan.

Saisuresh Krishnakumaran and Xiaojin Zhu. 2007. Hunting elusive metaphors using lexical resources. In Xiaofei Lu and Anna Feldman, editors, *Computational Approaches to Figurative Language, Workshop at HLT/NAACL 2007*, Rochester, NY.

George Lakoff and Mark Johnson. 1980. *Metaphors We Live By*. University of Chicago Press, Chicago, IL, 2003 edition.

George Lakoff and Mark Turner. 1989. *More Than Cool Reason: A Field Guide to Poetic Metaphor*. University of Chicago Press, Chicago and London.

George Lakoff. 1993. The contemporary theory of metaphor. In A. Ortony, editor, *Metaphor and thought, 2nd. ed.*, pages 202–251. Cambridge Univ Press, New York.

James H. Martin. 1990. *A Computational Model of Metaphor Interpretation*. Acad Press, San Diego, CA.

Zachary J. Mason. 2004. CorMet: a computational, corpus-based conventional metaphor extraction system. *Comp Ling*, 30(1):23–44, March.

Andrew Ortony. 1980. Some psycholinguistic aspects of metaphor. In R.P. Honeck and H.R. Robert, editors, *Cog and Fig Lang*, pages 69–83. Erlbaum Associates, Hillsdale, NJ.

Wendy Oxman-Michelli. 1991. Critical thinking as creativity. Technical Report SO 023 597, Montclair State, Institute for Critical Thinking, Montclair, NJ.

Martha Palmer, Paul Kingsbury, and Daniel Gildea. 2005. The Proposition Bank: An annotated corpus of semantic roles. *Comp Ling*, 31(1):71–106, March.

Michael J. Reddy. 1969. A semantic approach to metaphor. In *Chicago Linguistic Society Collected Papers*, pages 240–251. Chicago Univ Press, Chicago.

Philip Resnik. 1993. *Selection and Information: A Class-Based Approach to Lexical Relationships*. Dissertation, University of Pennsylvania, Department of Computer and Information Science.

Lei Shi and Rada Mihalcea. 2004. Open text semantic parsing using FrameNet and WordNet. In *Demonstration Papers at HLT-NAACL 2004*, pages 19–22, Boston. Assoc for Computational Linguistics.

Daniel Sleator and Davy Temperley. 1993. Parsing English with a Link Grammar. In *Proc Third International Workshop on Parsing Technologies*, pages 277–292.

Engineering Linguistic Creativity: Bird Flight and Jet Planes

Pablo Gervás
Universidad Complutense de Madrid
c/ Profesor García Santesmases s/n
Madrid, 28040, Spain
pgervas@sip.ucm.es

Abstract

Man achieved flight by studying how birds fly, and yet the solution that engineers came up with (jet planes) is very different from the one birds apply. In this paper I review a number of efforts in automated story telling and poetry generation, identifying which human abilities are being modelled in each case. In an analogy to the classic example of bird-flight and jet planes, I explore how the computational models relate to (the little we know about) human performance, what the similarities are between the case for linguistic creativity and the case for flight, and what the analogy might have to say about artificial linguistic creativity if it were valid.

1 Introduction

The achievement of flight by man is often used as an example of how engineering practice may lead to the successful emulation of behaviours observed in nature. It is also used to illustrate the idea that a successful engineering solution (such as a jet plane) need not always mirror faithfully the natural phenomenon which inspired it (the flight of birds).

The task of engineering solutions for linguistic creativity is made difficult by an incomplete understanding of how we manage language and how we achieve creativity. Nevertheless, over the past few years a large research effort has been devoted to exploring issues such as computational creativity, automated story telling, or poetry generation. In these cases, there is also a combination of a naturally occurring source phenomenon and a set of engineering techniques that provide an emulation of it.

In this paper I review a number of such research and development efforts that I have been involved in or studied in detail, paying particular attention to identifying which traits of human activity are being modelled in each case. In an analogy to the classic example of bird-flight and jet planes, I explore how the computational models of linguistic creativity relate to (the little we know about) human performance, what the similarities are between the case for linguistic creativity and the case for flight, and what the analogy might have to say about artificial linguistic creativity if it were valid.

2 Creativity at Different Levels of Linguistic Decision

Creativity is a tricky word because it can mean different things to different people. There seems to be a historical reason for this, in as much as the actual word we now use seems to have been invented in the 19th century in an attempt to cover the different concepts of innovation that were accepted in art and science (Weiner, 2000). As it is very difficult to make progress without a minimal agreement on what we are talking about, I will set off with an attempt to clarify what I refer to when I use the word in what follows. This is not intended to be prescriptive of how it should be used or descriptive of what other people may mean when they use it. And it is not meant to be exhaustive.[1] The goal here is to provide a brief sketch for readers to have a general idea of what is being talked about.

[1] Interested readers can refer to (Gervás, 2009) for a more detailed discussion of my personal view on creativity.

Proceedings of the NAACL HLT 2010 Second Workshop on Computational Approaches to Linguistic Creativity, pages 23–30,
Los Angeles, California, June 2010.

For me creativity suggests the idea of someone (a *creator*) generating something (an *output*) that is somehow new, but also somewhat unexpected or different from what others might have produced. This output should satisfy some *goal*, though in many cases the particular goal implied is not altogether clear. The expectation of novelty implicitly brings in a second agent (an *audience* which usually involves more than one individual) that perceives or evaluates the result.

When used in different contexts, the word creativity acquires different meanings by virtue of involving different concepts of author, product, goal, or audience. The assumption that there is a generic framework common to all the different cases should be taken with a pinch of salt, as commonalities may not go far beyond this basic sketch.

It may seem that restricting the study to linguistic creativity simplifies the issue. Surely once the domain is constrained to linguistic outputs, the description of creativity should indeed boil down to a simple common framework. This assumption may also be risky, as I discuss below.

There are several possible levels of decision at which the final form of a sentence is shaped. At any (or all) of these it is possible to exercise creativity in the sense described above. At the level of phonetics, the way letters are put together to make sounds can be explored in search of pleasing uses of rhyme, internal rhyme or alliteration, as done in sound poetry (Hultberg, 1993). If one considers rhythm, the stress patterns of words may shape the stress pattern of a sentence or a text into rhythms that are uncommon in the language, or in existing poetry, as Poe claims to have done in "The Raven" (Poe, 1846). With respect to lexical choice, the actual words chosen for the text may be words that the user does not know but which actually convey a certain meaning to the reader, as done by Lewis Carrol in the poem "Jabberwocky" (Carrol, 1872).

For other levels of decisions, such as syntax, semantics or narrative, it is more difficult to pinpoint specific examples of creative uses, because instances occur in larger contexts and because they occur much more frequently. They can be considered of two different kinds: those in which the main objective is the communication of a certain message or information, and those geared towards obtaining a pleasing effect of some sort. The first kind occurs for instance when a speaker in a hurry waives the rules of correct syntax in his effort to get his message accross briefly. In going beyond the accepted rules, such a speaker may be deemed to be behaving creatively. This type of linguistic creativity (say, corner-cutting creative communication) is worth exploring in detail, but it would require access to enough samples of specific instances of the phenomenon to provide starting material. The second kind, in contrast, tend to get explicitly recorded for this pleasing effect to be available at later times, and they provide an easier starting point for a study of this sort.

A number of examples of linguistic creativity of the second kind were reviewed in (Gervás, 2002). This study showed that creative behaviour does not occur in the same degree across all levels. Creativity applied simultaneously at several linguistic levels can be counterproductive for communication if abused. Instead, a conservative approach in some levels is required for a successful interpretation of creative innovations at other levels. An additional problem that would have to be tackled is the extent to which the interaction between the theories for the different levels complicates the picture significantly. Intuition suggests that it will to a considerable extent. Creativity may operate at each of the levels of decision involved in linguistic production, but it may interact between different levels in ways that are not evident.

Under this light, we can see that even within the realm of linguistic creativity we seem to be faced with a broad range of different types of creativity, with different concepts of product and goal, giving shape to widely differing phenomena. In the hope of reducing even further the scope of the problem, I will concentrate more specifically on instances where a computer program is written to generate pieces of text that, when produced by a human author, would be interpreted to have deliberate aspirations of creativity.

3 Some Automatic Creators in the Literary Field

An exhaustive study of existing automatic creators of this kind would take more space than I have available here. The selection below must not be understood to be exhaustive. It is not even intended to indicate that the particular creators mentioned constitute the most significant efforts in the field. I have selected only a few for purposes of illustration, and I have chosen examples where relevant features of the corresponding human processes have been considered. There are two main fields where computer programs attempt to generate literary material: storytelling programs and poetry generators. Again, a difference in genre introduces differences in product, goal and evaluation criteria, which leads to the application of different construction processes, so I will review each field separately.

3.1 Automatic Story Tellers

Research on storytelling systems has experienced considerable growth over the years. Although it has never been a popular research topic, nonetheless it has received sustained attention over the years by a dedicated community of researchers. In recent years the number of systems developed has increased significantly. The body of work resulting from these efforts has identified a significant number of relevant issues in storytelling. Successive systems have identified particular elements in stories that play a role in the process of generation. Only a few illustrative examples will be mentioned here.

It is clear that planning has been central to efforts of modelling storytelling for a long time. Most of the existing storytelling systems feature a planning component of some kind, whether as a main module or as an auxiliary one. TALESPIN (Meehan, 1977), AUTHOR (Dehn, 1981), UNIVERSE (Lebowitz, 1983), MINSTREL (Turner, 1993) and Fabulist (Riedl, 2004), all include some representation of goals and/or causality, though each of them uses it differently in the task of generating stories. An important insight resulting from this work (originally formulated by (Dehn, 1981) but later taken up by others) was the distinction between goals of the characters in the story or goals of the author. This showed that planning is a highly relevant tool for storytelling, both at the level of how the coherence of stories can be represented and how the process of generating them is related to goals and causality.

Another aspect that is obviously relevant for storytelling is emotion. This has been less frequently addressed in automatic storytellers, but has an outstanding champion in the MEXICA system. MEXICA (Pérez y Pérez, 1999) was a computer model designed to study the creative process in writing in terms of the cycle of engagement and reflection (Sharples, 1999), which presents a description of writing understood as a problem-solving process where the writer is both a creative thinker and a designer of text. MEXICA was designed to generate short stories about the Mexicas (also wrongly known as Aztecs), and it is a flexible tool where the user can set the value of different parameters to constrain the writing process and explore different aspects of story generation. An important aspect of MEXICA is that it takes into account emotional links and tensions between the characters as means for driving and evaluating ongoing stories. The internal representation that MEXICA uses for its stories (a Story World Context) is built incrementally as a story is either read or produced (the system can do both, as it learns its craft from a set of previous stories). This representation keeps track of emotional links and emotional tensions between characters. These elements are represented as preconditions and postconditions of the set of available actions. The system evaluates the quality of a partial draft for a story in terms of the the rising and falling shape of the arc of emotional tensions that can be computed from this information.

In general, most storytelling systems, being AI-style programs, can be said to operate by searching a space of solutions, guided by a traversal function that leads to new points in the space and an evaluation function that rates each point of the space in terms of quality. In general, most systems concentrate on the development and innovation efforts in the function for generating new stories (the traversal function), hoping that the candidates generated will progressively get better. However, human authors seem to learn their craft mostly by learning to distinguish good stories from bad stories (which would involve focusing more on the evaluation function). A fairly recent proposal (Gervás and León,) describes a story generation system that outputs new stories obtained by exploring a restricted conceptual space under the guidance of a set of evaluation rules. The interesting feature in this system is that it uses exhaustive enumeration of the search space as its only exploration procedure, and relies solely on its evaluation rules to identify good stories. This is a direct application of the generate & test paradigm of problem solving. This system also models the way in which the evaluation rules can evolve over time, leading to the production of new results.

3.2 Automatic Poetry Generators

Automatic poetry generators differ significantly from storytellers in two aspects: they are expected to satisfy very specific metric restrictions (in terms of number of syllables per line, and position of stressed syllables within the line) on the form of the output text (which story tellers do not usually take into account), and they are allowed a certain poetic licence which boils down to relaxing, sometimes quite dramatically, any expectations of meaning or coherence in the output (which are fundamental for storytellers). As a result, there is a larger sample of poetry generators. The review presented below attempts to cover some of the basic techniques that have been used as underlying technologies.

The generate & test paradigm of problem solving has also been widely applied in poetry generators. Because metric restrictions are reasonably easy to model computationally, very simple generation solutions coupled with an evaluation function for metric constraints are likely to produce acceptable results (given an assumption of poetic licence as regards to the content). An example of this approach is the early version of the WASP system (Gervás, 2000). Initial work by Manurung (Manurung, 1999) also applied a generate & test approach based on chart generation, but added an important restriction: that poems to be generated must aim for some specific semantic content, however vaguely defined at the start of the composition process. This constitutes a significant restriction on the extent of poetic licence allowed.

Manurung went on to develop in his Phd thesis (Manurung, 2003) an evolutionary solution for this problem. Evolutionary solutions seem particularly apt to model this process as they bear certain similarities with the way human authors may explore several possible drafts in parallel, progressively editing them while they are equally valuable, focusing on one of them when it becomes better valued than others, but returning to others if later modifications prove them more interesting.

Another important tactic that human authors are known to use is that of reusing ideas, structures, or phrasings from previous work in new results. This is very similar to the AI technique of Case-Based Reasoning (CBR). Some poetry generators have indeed explored the use of this technique as a basic generation mechanism. An evolution of the WASP system (Gervás, 2001) used CBR to build verses for an input sentence by relying on a case base of matched pairs of prose and verse versions of the same sentence. Each case was a set of verses associated with a prose paraphrase of their content. An input sentence was used to query the case base and the structure of the verses of the best-matching result was adapted into a verse rendition of the input. This constituted a different approach to hardening the degree of poetic licence required to deem the outputs acceptable (the resulting verses should have a certain relation to the input sentence).

Another important mechanism that has been employed by automatic poets is grammar-based generation. By using a grammar to produce grammatically correct combinations of words, the results obtained start to resemble understandable sentences. As Chomsky mentioned in 1957, the fact that a sentence is grammatically correct does not imply that it will be interpretable. However, in the context of automatically generated poetry, sentences like Chomsky's classic counterexample ("Colorless green ideas sleep furiously") acquire a special interest, as they provide both a sense of validity (due to their syntactic correctness) and a sense of adventure (due to the impossibility of pinpointing a specific meaning for them). On reading such sentences, the human mind comes up with a number of conflicting interpretations, none fully compatible with its literal meaning. This multiplicity of shifting meanings is very atractive in the light of modern theories about the role of reader interpretation in the reading process.

In 1984 William Chamberlain published a book of poems called "The Policeman's Beard is Half Constructed" (Chamberlain, 1981). In the preface, Chamberlain claimed that all the book (but the preface) had been written by a computer program. The program, called RACTER, managed verb conjugation and noun declension, and it could assign certain elements to variables in order to reuse them periodically (which gave an impression of thematic continuity). Although few details are provided regarding the implementation, it is generally assumed that RACTER employed grammar-based generation. The poems in Chamberlain's book showed a degree of sophistication that many claim would be impossible to obtain using only grammars, and it has been suggested that a savvy combination of grammars, carefully-crafted templates and heavy filtering of a very large number of results may have been employed.

The use of n-grams to model the probability of certain words following on from others has proven to be another useful tecnique. An example of poetry generation based on this is the cybernetic poet developed by Ray Kurtzweil. RKCP (Ray Kurtzweils Cybernetic Poet)[2] is trained on a selection of poems by an author or authors and it creates from them a language model of the work of those authors. From this model, RKCP can produce original poems which will have a style similar to the author on which they were trained. The generation process is controlled by a series of additional parameters, for instance, the type of stanza employed. RKCP includes an algorithm to avoid generating poems too close to the originals used during its training, and certain algorithms to maintain thematic coherence over a given poem. Over specific examples, it could be seen that the internal coherence of given verses was good, but coherence within sentences that spanned more than one verse was not so impressive.

4 Discussion

The selection of automatic creators reviewed above provides a significant sample of human abilities related with linguistic creativity that have been modelled with reasonable success. These include: the ability to recognise causality and use plans as skeletons for the backbone of a text, the ability to identify emotional reactions and evaluate a story in terms of emotional arcs, the ability to relax restrictions at the time of building and delay evaluation until fuller results have been produced, the ability to iterate over a draft applying successive modifications in search of a best fit, the ability to measure metric forms, the ability to reuse the structures of texts we liked in the past, the ability to rely on grammars for generating valid text, and the ability to use n-grams to produce a stream of text with surface form in a certain style. This list of abilities is doubtless not exhaustive, but it covers a broad range of aspects. The important idea is that although existing systems have identified and modelled these abilities, very few have considered more than one or two of them simultaneously. And yet intuition suggests that human authors are likely to apply a combination of all of these (and probably many more additional ones that have not been modelled yet) even in their simplest efforts.

It may pay to look in more detail at the set of tools that we have identified, with a view to considering how they might be put together in a single system if we felt so inclined. The engagement and reflection model (Sharples, 1999) may provide a useful framework for this purpose. Sharples' concept of engagement seems to correspond with the ability to generate a new instance of a given artefact, without excessive concern to the quality or fitness for purpose of the partial result at any intermediate stage of the process. According to this view, planners, case-based reasoning, grammars, or n-gram models can provide reasonable implementations of procedures for engagement. The concept of reflection captures the need to evaluate the material generated during engagement. Abilities like identifying emotional reactions and evaluating a story in terms of emotional arcs, or measuring metric forms would clearly have a role to play during reflection. However, it is important to consider that we are looking at a number of possible mechanisms for use in engagement, together with a number of possible mechanisms for use in reflection. This does indeed have a place in the general scheme proposed by Sharples. Sharples proposes a cyclic process moving through two different phases: engagement and reflection. During the reflection phase, the generated material is revised in a three step process of reviewing, contemplating and planning the result. During reviewing the result is read, minor edits may be carried out, but most important it is interpreted to represent "the procedures enacted during composition as explicit knowledge". Contemplation involves the process of operating on the results of this interpretation. Planning uses the results of contemplation to create plans or

[2] http://www.kurzweilcyberart.com/poetry/rkcp_overview.php3

intentions to guide the next phase of engagement. The evidence that we have presented so far suggests that a specific mechanism (or maybe more than one) may have been chosen to be used during a particular cycle of engagement. The process of reviewing mentioned by Sharples might simply be one of explicitly considering the choice of mechanism to use in engagement. The process of contemplating might be an application of the full set of evaluation mechanisms particular to reflection. The process of planning could be a complex process which would include among other things a decision of whether to change the engagement mechanism in use (or the configuration of any parameters it may need), and which mechanism to apply in each situation.

But we should not only study how closely automatic creators resemble human ones, assuming any divergence is a negative factor. Particular attention must be paid to the question of whether certain characteristics of human creativity are necessary conditions for creativity or simply the ingenious solution that makes it possible for the human mind while remaining within its limitations. This is particularly important if one is to consider modelling creativity in computer systems, which have different limitations, but also different advantages.

Humans have limited memory. Many of the solutions they seem to apply (such as providing constraints over a generative system so that it generates only "appropriate" solutions) are intended to avoid problems arising from the large amount of memory that would be required to consider all possible solutions provided by the generative system. But computers do not usually have the same problem. Computers can store and consider a much large number of solutions. This has in the past been the big advantage presented by computers over people. It is such a significant advantage that, for some tasks such as chess playing, computers can perform better by computing all options and evaluating them all (very fast) than people can by using intelligent heuristics.

Though little definite is known about how the brain works, it seems to follow a highly parallel approach to computation. This is not true of most modern day computers. The most widely extended model for modern computers is the Von Neumann architecture, a computer design model that uses a single processing unit and a single separate storage structure to hold both instructions and data. Over this simple model, subsequent layers of abstraction may be built, resulting in very complex models of performance as perceived by a human user running the computer. Many of these complex behaviours (such as, for instance, evolutionary problem solving techniques) have often been considered prime candidates for simulating creative behaviour in computers on the grounds that they implement a parallel search method, but they are reckoned to be slow, taking a long time to produce results. The lack of speed is highy influenced by the fact that, when run on computers with a Von Neumann architecture, each possible solution must be built and evaluated sequentially by the underlying single processing unit. If any computational solution based on parallel search methods shows merit for emulating creativity, it should not be discounted until it has been tested over hardware that allows it to operate in a really parallel manner, and instances of these are becoming more and more popular. Nowadays it has become more difficult to buy a new computer without finding it has at least two cores. For gaming consoles, this trend has gone even further, with the new generations sporting up to nine processing units.

5 Our Latest Efforts

Although the aim of the paper is not to report original work, a brief description of my ongoing work constitutes an example of the type of system that can be considered along the lines described above. The WASP poetry generator is still going strong. Only recently a selection of 10 poems produced by WASP has been published in a book about the possibilities of computers writing love poems (Gervás, 2010). The version of WASP used here is more advanced than previous ones, and some of the ideas outlined in the discussion have been introduced as modifications on earlier designs.

This version of WASP operates as a set of families of automatic experts: one family of content generators (which generate a flow of text that is taken as a starting point by the poets), one family of poets (which try to convert flows of text into poems in given strophic forms), one family of judges (which evaluate different aspects that are considered important), and one family of revisers (which apply modifications to the drafts they receive, each one oriented to correct a type of problem, or to modify the draft in a specific way). These families work in a coordinated manner like a cooperative society of readers/critics/editors/writers. All together they generate a population of drafts over which they all operate, modifying it and pruning it in an evolutionary manner over a pre-established number of generations of drafts, until a final version, the best valued effort of the lot, is chosen.

The overall style of the resulting poems is strongly determined by the accumulated sources used to train the content generators, which are mostly n-gram based. The poems presented in the book were produced with content generators trained on collections of texts by Federico García Lorca, Miguel Hernández and a selection of Sixteenth Century Spanish poets. Readers familiar with the sources can detect similarities in vocabulary, syntax and theme. A specific judge is in charge of penalising instances of excessive similarity with the sources, which then get pushed down in the ranking and tend not to emerge as final solutions.

The various judges assign scores on specific parameters (on poem length, on verse length, on rhyme, on stress patterns of each line, on similarity to the sources, fitness against particular strophic forms...) and an overall score for each draft is obtained by combining all individual scores received by the draft.

Poets operate mainly by deciding on the introduction of line breaks over the text they receive as input.

Revisers rely on scores assigned by judges to introduce changes to drafts. Modifications can be of several types: deletion of spans of text, substitution of spans for newly generated ones, word substitution, sentence elimination, and simple cross-over of fragments of poems to obtain new ones.

Because an initial draft produced by an n-gram based content generator is then processed many times over by poets and revisers, final results oscillate between surprising faithfulness to the sources and very radical surreal compositions.

6 Conclusions

In view of the material presented, and taking up the analogy between linguistic creativity and bird flight, we can say we are still trying to model birds. So far, we have only achieved small models of parts of birds. The various features of automatic creators that have been vaguely related to human abilities in section 4 are clearly tools that human writers apply in their daily task. Having systems that model these techniques, and testing how far each technique goes towards modelling human activity are steps forward. Bird's wings or bird's feathers do not fly, but having good models of them is crucial to understanding what makes flight possible.

Yet humans do not apply any of them in isolation, but rather rely on them as a set of tools and combine them at need to produce new material, using different combinations at different times. In the same way as research into flight considered how the parts of birds interact to achieve flight, in the realm of linguistic creativity more effort should be made to model the way in which humans combine different techniques and tools to achieve results. This could not have been done a few years back for lack of a valid set of tools to start from, but it is feasible now.

Aside from this positive optimistic analysis, there is a darker thought to keep in mind. Because we recognise that the models we are building at the current stage are only reproductions of parts of the whole mechanism, it would be unrealistic to demand of them that they exhibit right now creativity at the level of humans. As long as they focus on one aspect and leave out others, they are likely to perform poorly in the overall task when compared with their human couterparts. Yet even if they do not they are still worthy pursuits as initial and fundamental steps on which to build better solutions.

Once the various elements that contribute to the task have been identified and modelled with reasonable success, and the way in which they interact when humans apply them, a new universe of possibilities opens up. Future research should address the way in which humans apply these various elements, especially the way in which they combine some with others to achieve better results. In doing this, researchers should inform themselves with existing research on this subject in the fields of psychology, but also in the study of poetry, narratology and literary theory in general.

By doing this, it will become more likely that computer programs ever produce output comparable to that of human authors. Yet the overall goal should not just be to obtain a pastiche of specific human artifacts, indistinguishable from the corresponding human-produced versions. Jet planes are perfectly distinguishable from birds. Which does not mean they are worthless. Jet planes are different from birds because the engineering solutions that scientists found for achieving flight required different materials (metal rather than bone and feathers), different applications of the basic principles (static rather than flapping wings) and different means of propulsion (jet engines rather than muscle power). However, these departures from the original model have made the current solution capable of feats that are impossible for birds. Jet planes can fly much faster, much higher, and carrying much more weight than any bird known. Yet all this was made possible by trying to emulate birds. If we carry the analogy to its full extent, we should generally consider departures from human models of linguistic creativity wherever they result in methods better suited for computers. This is already being done. However, we should at some stage also start considering departures from the models for the output as generated by humans. I would say a second, more idealistic, purpose of computational creativity might be to look for things that machines can do that people cannot do, but which people might yet learn to appreciate.

Acknowledgments

The work reported in this paper was partially supported by the Ministerio de Educación y Ciencia (TIN2006-14433-C02-01, TIN2009-14659-C03-01).

References

L. Carrol. 1872. *Through the Looking-Glass and What Alice Found There.* Bo Ejeby Edition, Sweden.

W. Chamberlain. 1981. *The Policeman's Beard is Half Constructed.* Warner Books, New york.

Natalie Dehn. 1981. Story generation after tale-spin. In *In Proceedings of the International Joint Conference on Artificial Intelligence*, pages 16–18.

P. Gervás and León. Story generation driven by system-modified evaluation validated by human judges. In *Proc. of the First International Conference on Computational Creativity.*

P. Gervás. 2000. WASP: Evaluation of different strategies for the automatic generation of spanish verse. In *Proceedings of the AISB-00 Symposium on Creative & Cultural Aspects of AI*, pages 93–100.

P. Gervás. 2001. An expert system for the composition of formal spanish poetry. *Journal of Knowledge-Based Systems*, 14(3-4):181–188.

P. Gervás. 2002. Linguistic creativity at different levels of decision in sentence production. In *Proceedings of the AISB 02 Symposium on AI and Creativity in Arts and Science*, pages 79–88.

P. Gervás. 2009. Computational approaches to storytelling and creativity. *AI Magazine*, 30(3):49–62.

P. Gervás. 2010. Diez poemas emocionales generados por un computador. In D. Cañas and C. González Tardón, editors, *¿Puede un computador escribir un poema de amor?*, pages 189–196. Editorial Devenir.

T. Hultberg. 1993. *Literally Speaking: sound poetry & text-sound composition.* Bo Ejeby Edition, Sweden.

M. Lebowitz. 1983. Story-telling as planning and learning. In *International Joint Conference on Artificial Intelligence*, volume 1.

H. M. Manurung. 1999. Chart generation of rhythm-patterned text. In *Proc. of the First International Workshop on Literature in Cognition and Computers.*

H. M. Manurung. 2003. *An evolutionary algorithm approach to poetry generation.* Ph.D. thesis, University of Edimburgh, Edimburgh, UK.

James R. Meehan. 1977. TALE-SPIN, an interactive program that writes stories. In *In Proceedings of the Fifth International Joint Conference on Artificial Intelligence*, pages 91–98.

R. Pérez y Pérez. 1999. *MEXICA: A Computer Model of Creativity in Writing.* Ph.D. thesis, The University of Sussex.

Edgar Allan Poe. 1846. The philosophy of composition. *Graham's Magazine*, XXVIII(28):163–167.

M. Riedl. 2004. *Narrative Planning: Balancing Plot and Character.* Ph.D. thesis, Department of Computer Science, North Carolina State University.

Mike Sharples. 1999. *How We Write: Writing As Creative Design.* Routledge, June.

Scott R. Turner. 1993. *Minstrel: a computer model of creativity and storytelling.* Ph.D. thesis, University of California at Los Angeles, Los Angeles, CA, USA.

R. Weiner. 2000. *Creativity & beyond : cultures, values, and change.* State University of New York Press, Albany, NY.

An alternate approach towards meaningful lyric generation in Tamil

Ananth Ramakrishnan A
AU-KBC Research Centre
MIT Campus of Anna University
Chennai, India
ananthrk@au-kbc.org

Sobha Lalitha Devi
AU-KBC Research Centre
MIT Campus of Anna University
Chennai, India
sobha@au-kbc.org

Abstract

This paper presents our on-going work to improve the lyric generation component of the Automatic Lyric Generation system for the Tamil Language. An earlier version of the system used an n-gram based model to generate lyrics that match the given melody. This paper identifies some of the deficiencies in the melody analysis and text generation components of the earlier system and explains the new approach used to tackle those drawbacks. The two central approaches discussed in this paper are: (1) An improved mapping scheme for matching melody with words and (2) Knowledge-based Text Generation algorithm based on an existing Ontology and Tamil Morphology Generator.

1 Introduction

In an attempt to define poetry (Manurung, 2004), provides three properties for a natural language artifact to be considered a poetic work, viz., Meaningfulness (M), Grammaticality (G) and Poeticness (P). A complete poetry generation system must generate texts that adhere to all the three properties. (Ananth et. al., 2009) explains an approach for automatically generating Tamil lyrics, given a melody, which attempts to generate meaningful lyrics that match the melody.

The existing approach (Ananth et. al., 2009) to automatically generate Tamil lyrics that match the given tune in *ABC* format (Gonzato, 2003) involves two steps. The first step is to analyze the input melody and output a series of possible syllable patterns in *KNM* representation scheme - a scheme for representing all words in the language, where, K stands for *Kuril* (**(C)V**, where V is a short vowel), N stands for *Nedil* (**(C)V**, where V is a long vowel) and M stands for *Mei* or *Ottru* (consonants) - that match the given melody, along with tentative word and sentence boundary. This melody analysis system was trained with sample film songs and their corresponding lyrics collected from the web. The tunes were converted to *ABC* Notation (Gonzato, 2003) and their lyrics were represented in *KNM* scheme. The trained model was then used to label the given input melody.

The subsequent step uses a Sentence Generator module to generate lines that match the given syllable pattern with words satisfying the following constraints: a) Words should match the syllable pattern and b) The sequence of words should have a meaning. This was achieved by using n-Gram models learnt from a Tamil text corpus.

Though the system manages to generate sentences that match the syllable pattern, it has the following limitations:

1) When no words are found matching a given syllable pattern, alternate patterns that are close to the given pattern, as suggested by the Edit Distance Algorithm, are considered. This algorithm treats the syllable patterns as strings for finding close patterns and hence, can provide choices that do not agree with the input melody.
2) The Sentence Generation is based on the n-Gram model learnt from a text corpus. This can result in sentences that do not have a coherent meaning. Also, since only bi-grams are considered, it can generate sentences that are ungrammatical due to Person-Number-Gender (PNG) agreement issues.

This paper is an attempt to propose alternate approaches in order to overcome the above limitations.

Proceedings of the NAACL HLT 2010 Second Workshop on Computational Approaches to Linguistic Creativity, pages 31–39,
Los Angeles, California, June 2010.

2 Limitations of existing approach

2.1 Finding close matches to syllable patterns

In the existing system, when no words are found matching the given syllable pattern (either due to a small corpus or rarity of the pattern), the closest patterns are considered as alternatives. The closest match to a given syllable pattern is generated based on the Edit Distance algorithm. For example, if the input sequence is given as "NKN" (*long vowel - short vowel - long vowel*) and if no words are found matching NKN, closest matches for NKN are generated. Thus, if an edit distance of 1 is considered, the alternate pattern choices are "KKN", "NKM", "NNN", "NMN", etc. However, not all of these syllable patterns can fit the original music notes.

As an example, consider the Tamil word "*thA-ma-rai*" (*lotus*) that fits the pattern NKN. Suppose no words that match the pattern NKN was present in the corpus and other close patterns were opted for, we get:

Pat.	Word	Meaning	Match
KKN	*tha-va-Lai*	*Frog*	No match
NKM	*thA-ba-m*	*Longing*	No match
NNN	*kO-sA-lai*	*Cow Hut*	Close Match
NMN	*pA-p-pA*	*Child*	No match

Table 1. Alternative patterns for "NKN"

None of the above words can be used in the place of "*thA-ma-rai*", a good fit for a NKN pattern, as they don't *phonetically* match (except for a close-but-not-exact "*kO-sA-lai"*) and hence cannot be used as part of the lyric without affecting the intended melody.

2.2 Ungrammatical or meaningless generation

The Sentence Generation algorithm was based on the n-Gram model built from a text corpus. Given that n-Gram based generation schemes have in-built bias towards shorter strings, it can end-up generating meaningless and ungrammatical sentences. As observed in (Ananth et.al., 2009), we can get sentences such as:

அவன் நடந்து சென்றாள்

(avan-He-3sm nadandhu-walk sendrAlY-3sf)*
(He reached by walking)

Here, the subject *avan (He),* which is a 3rd person, singular, masculine noun, does not agree with the verb *sendrAlY* , which is 3rd person, singular, feminine. Thus, the noun and the verb do not agree on the gender. The correct sentence should be:

அவன் நடந்து சென்றான்

(*avan-3sm nadandhu sendrAn*-3sm)

This is happening because the bi-gram score for நடந்து சென்றாள் could be greater than நடந்து சென்றான்.

Similar disagreements can happen for other aspects such as person or number. Though performing a joint probability across words would help in reducing such errors, it would slow down the generation process.

In addition to the above ungrammatical generation problem, the system can also generate meaningless sentences. Though, some of them can be considered as a *poetic license*, most of them were just non-sensical. For example, consider the following sentence generated by the n-Gram sentence generation system:

* அது இது என்

(adhu-that idhu-this en-my)
(*that this my)*

The above sentence does not convey any coherent meaning.

2.3 Ability to control theme/choice of words

Given the nature of the Sentence generation algorithm, it is not possible for the program to hand-pick specific words and phrases. That is, the whole generation process is guided by the probability values and hence it is not possible to bias the algorithm to produce utterances belonging to a particular theme.

In the subsequent sections, we explain the alternative approaches to tackle the above limitations.

3 Closest Syllable Patterns

The existing approach uses the *KNM Notation* for representing all words in the language. This phonetic representation is at the most basic level, i.e., alphabets, and hence can be used to represent all words in the language. The *KNM notation* is generated by the melody analyzer and is used throughout the system for generating sentences. Though this representation scheme is at the most basic level, it does not help in cases where we are looking for alternate or close matches. Thus, we need to come up with a representation scheme at a higher level of abstraction that will help us in providing valid choices without compromising the requirements of the melody. To this end, we hereby propose to use elements from classic poetry metric rules in Tamil Grammar (Bala et. al., 2003) as defined in the oldest Tamil Grammar work, *Tholkappiyam* (Tholkappiyar, 5th Century B.C.).

3.1 Meter in classical Tamil Poetry

Meter is the basic rhythmic structure of a verse and the basic term that refers to Tamil meter is *pA*. Each line in the poem is called an *adi,* which, in turn, is made up of a certain number of metrical feet known as the *ceer (*words/tokens*)*. Each *ceer* is composed of a certain metrical units called *asai* (syllables) which are made up of letters (vowels and consonants) that have certain intrinsic length/duration, known as *mAthirai*. The above entities are known as the core structural components of a Tamil poem (Rajam, 1992)

The basic metrical unit *asai* is mostly based on vowel length. There are two basic types of *asai*: *nEr asai* (straightness) and *niRai asai* (in a row; array). The *nEr asai* has the pattern **(C)V(C)(C)** and *niRai asai*, **(C)VCV(C)(C)**. These longest-matching basic *asai* patterns are expanded to represent non-monosyllabic words, but for our needs, we use these two basic *asai* patterns for the new representation scheme.

3.2 *asai*-based Representation Scheme

In the new representation scheme, the constituents of the KNM representation scheme are converted to *nEr* or *niRai asai* before being sent to the Sentence Generator module. The Sentence Generator module, in turn, makes use of this new representation scheme for picking words as well as for finding alternatives. In this new representation scheme, a *nEr asai* is represented as *Ne* and a *niRai asai* is represented as *Ni*.

The following table illustrates the mapping required for converting between the two representation schemes:

KNM Representation	***asai* representation**
K	*Ne*
KM(0….2)	*Ne*
N	*Ne*
NM(0…2)	*Ne*
KK	*Ni*
KKM(0…2)	*Ni*
KN	*Ni*
KNM(0…2)	*Ni*

Table 2. KNM to *asai* representation

For example, an output line such as, for example, "KK KK KKK" in the old representation scheme will be converted as "*Ni Ni NiNe*" in the new representation based on *asai*. This means that the line should contain three *ceer*(words/tokens) and the first word should be a *nirai asai*, second word should be a *nirai asai* and the third word contains two syllables with a *nirai asai* followed by *nEr asai*.

This new representation scheme helps in coming up with alternatives without affecting the metrical needs of the melody as the alternatives have the same *mAthirai* (length/duration). Thus, if we are given a pattern such as "***NiNe***", we have several valid choices such as "KKK" (originally given), "KKMK", "KKMKM", "KKN", "KKMN" and "KKMNM". We can use words that match any of the above patterns without compromising the duration imposed by the original music note. This way of choosing alternatives is much better than using the Edit Distance algorithm as it is based on the original meter requirements as against matching string patterns.

To use the previous example of "*thA-ma-rai*" (*lotus*) (NKN) in this new representation scheme, we get, "***NeNi***" and all the following words will match:

Word	KNM scheme
nE-ra-lai (straight wave)	NKN
Sa-nj-nja-la-m (doubt)	KMKKM
Ma-ng-ka-la-m (auspicious)	KMKKM
a-m-bi-kai (goddess)	KMKN
vE-ng-ka-ta-m (Venkatam – a name)	NMKKM

Table 3. NKN alternatives using *asai* representation

The above (valid) choices such as KMKKM, NMKKM, etc. are not possible with just using the Edit Distance algorithm. Thus, the architecture of the system now consists of a new component for this conversion (Figure 1)

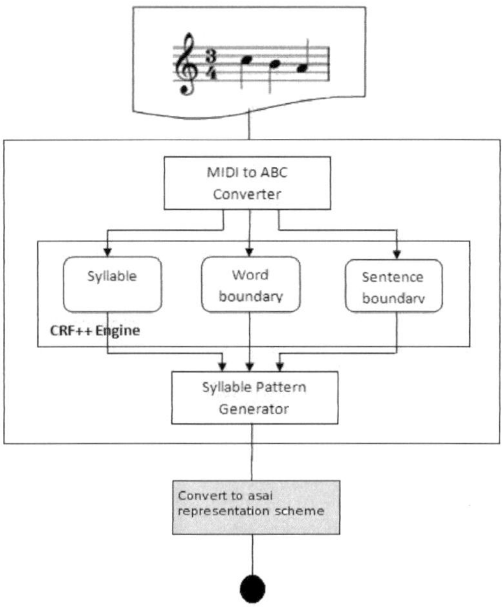

Figure 1. System Approach with new *ASAI* converter

4 Knowledge-based Sentence Generation

The goal of the Sentence Generation module is to generate sentences matching the input pattern given in the new *asai* representation scheme. The existing system generated sentences based on the n-Gram language model created from a text corpus of poems and film songs. However, as explained earlier, this can result in ungrammatical or meaningless sentences being generated. In order to overcome this limitation, the Sentence Generation module is completely overhauled using a knowledge-based approach. A Tamil Morphology generator component, built in-house, is used to generate grammatically correct sentences from this knowledge base.

4.1 Knowledge Base

The knowledge base consists of: (a) set of verbs along with their selectional restriction rules (b) hand-coded sub-categorization Ontology with nouns and (c) list of adjectives and adverbs learned from a text corpus.

4.1.1 Verbs and Selectional Restrictions

Selectional restriction is defined as the right of the verb to select its arguments. Verb is the nucleus of a sentence and has the nature of choosing its arguments. Any particular verb can take its arguments only according to its selectional restriction constraints. When these constraints are violated, the meaning of the sentence is affected. This violation of selectional restriction rules may lead to semantically wrong sentences or figurative usages. Correctness of a sentence not only depends on the syntactic correctness, but also with the semantic interpretation of the sentence.

4.1.2 Syntactic Classification

Verbs can be broadly classified into three divisions, viz., monadic, dyadic and triadic verbs. Monadic verbs can have only one argument - the subject. Dyadic verbs can have two arguments - subject and object. Triadic verbs can take three arguments - subject, direct and indirect objects. But there is no strict rule that the triadic verbs should have all three arguments or the dyadic verbs should have the two arguments filled. There can be overlaps between these groups of verbs. Triadic verb can drop the indirect object and have a Prepositional Phrase (PP) attached with the sentence. Dyadic verb can drop the object and still give a valid sentence. The verbs are grouped according to the sub-categorization information of the subject and object nouns. The sub-categorization features are explained in the following section. At present, we are using only Monadic and Dyadic verbs for our sentence generation purposes.

4.1.3 Sub-Categorization

Sub-categorization features explain the nature of the noun. The subject and object nouns are analyzed using these features. These features may include the type of noun, its characteristics, state etc. Sub-categorization information includes the features such as [±animate], [±concrete], [±edible] etc.

Some of the features and the meanings are listed below:

[+animate]	All animals, human beings
[+human]	All human beings
[+female]	Animals/human beings of feminine gender
[+solid]	Things that are in solid state
[+vehicle]	All vehicles
[+concrete]	Things that physically exist
[-concrete]	Things that do not physically exist
[+edible]	Things that can be eaten
[-edible]	Things that cannot be eaten
[+movable]	Things that are movable
[-movable]	Things that are not movable

Table 4. Sub-categorization Features

4.1.4 Ontology of Nouns

The sub-categorization features are used in the formulation of general Ontology of Nouns. It is made with respect to the usage of language. The Ontology that is developed has the following salient features:

- It is a language-based Ontology originally developed for English and has been customized for Tamil
- Nodes in the Ontology are the actual sub-categorization features of Nouns
- It is made according to the use of nouns in the Tamil language
- Each node will have a list of nouns as entries for that node

The complete Ontology can be found in (Arulmozhi, et. al., 2006)

4.1.5 Contents of Knowledge Base

At present, the knowledge-base consists of 116 unique verbs, 373 selectional restriction rules and 771 Nouns in the Ontology.

The verbs list includes both cognitive as well as non-cognitive verbs. Examples of verbs include *pAr* (to see), *kelY* (to listen), *vA* (to come), *thEtu* (to search), *piti* (to catch), *po* (to go), *kal* (to learn), etc.

The selectional restriction rules are stored as follows:

Verb=>subject_category;subject_case=>object_category;object_case.

When a verb does not take any object, the keyword *[no_obj]* is used to denote the same. In addition to the subject and object categories, the rule also contains the appropriate case markers to be used for the subject and object nouns. This additional information is stored for use by the Morph Generation component.

Some examples of selectional restriction rules are given below:

pAr=>[+living,+animate,+vertebrate,+mammal,+human];NOM=>[no_obj]

pAr=>[+living,+animate,+vertebrate,+mammal,+human];NOM=>[+living,+animate,+vertebrate,+mammal,+human];ACC

piti=>[+living,+animate,+vertebrate,+mammal,+human];NOM=>[living,+concrete,+movable,+artifact,+solid,+instrument,-vehicle,+implements];NOM

piti=>[+living,+animate,+vertebrate,+mammal,+human];NOM=>[no_obj]

Here, *ACC, NOM, DAT*, etc. denote the case markers to be used for the subject and object nouns.

The 771 Nouns are stored across several files according to their position in the Ontology. An Ontology map is used to determine the list of nouns present in a particular node position.

4.1.6 Adjectives and Adverbs

In addition to the verbs and nouns mentioned above, the knowledge-base also contains a list of adjective-noun and adverb-verb bi-grams learnt from a text corpus. This information is used to augment the Sentence Generator with words from these POS categories.

4.2 Tamil Morphological Generator

Tamil is a densely agglutinative language and displays a unique structural formation of words by the addition of suffixes representing various senses or grammatical categories, to the roots or stems. The senses such as person, number, gender and case are linked to a noun root in an orderly fashion. The verbal categories such as transitive, causative, tense and person, number and gender are added to a verbal root or stem. Thus, with the given knowledge-base and a Tamil Morphological generator component one can generate grammatically correct sentences.

We use the Tamil Morphological Generator component (Menaka et. al., 2010) to generate inflections of subject/object nouns with appropriate number & case and the verbs with person, number and gender suffixes.

4.3 Sentence Generation

Given a line in *asai* representation scheme, the sentence generation module is responsible for generating a grammatically correct and meaningful sentence matching the given *asai* scheme. It achieves the same by using the knowledge-base along with the Tamil Morphology Generator component (Figure 2). In addition to the *asai* representation, the module also accepts the tense in which the sentence must be written. The rest of the parameters such as person, gender and case are automatically deduced by the module.

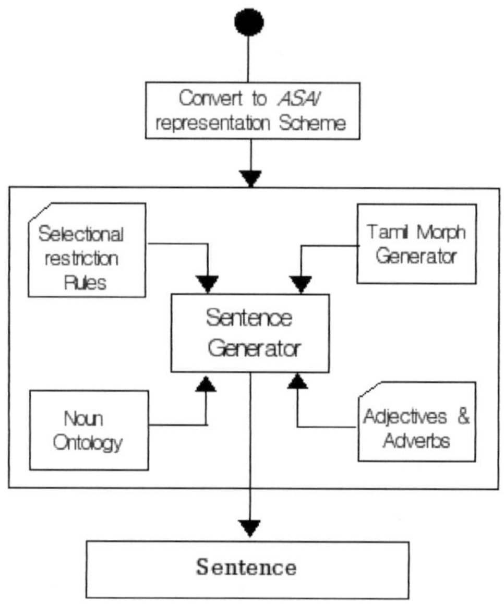

Figure 2. Sentence Generator module

The algorithm for generating a matching sentence is as follows:

1. Pick a selectional restriction rule, R in random

2. For each noun, SUB_N in subject_category of rule, R:

2.1 Guess the gender for SUB_N based on subject_category

2.2 For each noun, OBJ_N in object_category:

2.2.1 Use Morphology Generator component to get morphed nouns & verbs based on tense, person, gender and case.

2.2.2 Generate sentences of the form [SUB_N] [OBJ_N] [VERB]

2.2.3 Add adjectives or adverbs, if needed

2.2.4 Repeat words, if needed

2.2.4 Add to list of sentences generated

3. Check the list of sentences against the *asai* pattern. If matches, return sentence. Otherwise, go to step 1.

Table 5. Sentence Generation Algorithm

Details about steps such as matching against *asai* pattern, gender identification, word repetition and adding adjectives/adverbs are explained below.

4.3.1 Matching against *asai* pattern

The list of sentences generated from the module are compared against the given *asai* pattern. The matching could either be an exact match or a re-ordered match. That is, since Tamil is a relatively free word-order language, the generated sentence can also be re-ordered, if required, to match the given *asai* pattern. However, when adjectives or adverbs are added to the sentence, they need to maintain their position in front of the noun or verb respectively and hence they are not re-ordered. For now, we do not weight the sentences and hence return the first matching sentence.

4.3.2 Gender Identification

As noted in the algorithm, the gender needs to be automatically guessed. In Tamil, the gender of the subject is denoted by the appropriate suffix in the verb. If a personal pro-noun such as *nAnY* (I) or *nI* (you) is used as subject, then any of masculine or feminine gender can be used without affecting the grammatical correctness of the verb. In this case, the program uses the default value of masculine gender. If the subject is not a personal pronoun, the gender for the verb is guessed based on the subject_category of the subject noun. If the subject_category explicitly mentions [+human, +living, +female,…], then feminine gender is returned. If the subject_category explicitly mentions [+human, +living, -female,…], then masculine gender is returned. Otherwise, if [+human, +living,…] is present, but there is no explicit mention of +female or –female, it defaults to honorific suffix. In all other cases, neuter gender is returned.

4.3.3 Adding adjectives and adverbs

The Sentence Generator module using the selectional restriction rules can only create sentences of the form "*[subject] [object] [verb]*". However, typical lyrics will not always contain just three word sentences and thus, the ability to put more words in a sentence generated by our system is required. In such cases, a look-up list of adjectives and adverbs is used for filling the additional words required by the syllable pattern. This look-up list is generated from a POS-tagged text corpus from which the list of adjective-noun, adverb-verb bigrams are added to the look-up list. Whenever a sentence needs more than three words, this look-up list is consulted to generate sentences that add the relevant adjectives to subject or object nouns and relevant adverbs before the verb. Each possible combination of such sentences is generated and added to the list of sentences.

4.3.4 Word repetition

An additional approach to handle lines with more than three words is to repeat certain words already present in the "*[subject] [object] [verb]*" output. If an adjective or adverb is already added to the sentence, then preference for repetition is given to the adjective/adverb subject to the constraints of the input *asai* scheme. Otherwise, the verb is chosen for repetition. Finally, the subject and object nouns are considered.

5 Experiments

The goal of the experiment was to validate whether the sentences generated using the Knowledge-based approach are more grammatical and meaningful than the n-Gram approach. In order to test this hypothesis, a set of 10 syllable patterns was given to the old n-Gram system and 30 sentences were generated from them. The new knowledge-based approach was also given the syllable patterns and the resulting 32 sentences were collected. In order to avoid any bias, these 62 sentences were interleaved in a single document and this document was given to five human evaluators for scoring each sentence. The scoring methodology is as follows:

Score	Meaning
1	Incorrect
2	Grammatically perfect, but no meaning at all
3	Grammatically correct but only partially meaningful
4	Both Grammar and Meaning are only partially correct
5	Perfect

Table 6. Scoring methodology

Based on the scores given by the human evaluators, the sentences generated using the n-Gram approach scored an average of **2.06**, whereas the sentences generated using the knowledge-based approach scored an average of **4.13**. This clearly demonstrates that the new approach results in consistently more grammatical and meaningful sentences.

A break-down of statistics based on the scores given by each evaluator is given below (Table 7):

	E-1	*E-2*	*E-3*	*E-4*	*E-5*
Avg. Score (KB)*	4.5	4.38	4.06	4.09	3.63
Avg. Score (n-G)*	2.37	1	3.3	2.13	1.5
# Sentences scoring 5 (KB)	25	25	23	20	14
# Sentences scoring 5 (n-G)	6	0	14	1	0
# Sentences scoring 1 (KB)	2	0	7	4	7
# Sentences scoring 1 (n-G)	16	30	11	19	25

Table 7. Detailed Statistics

*KB = Knowledge-based approach and n-G = n-Gram based approach.

A subset of syllable patterns given to the system and the sentences generated by the system are given below:

Input	**NM KKMKMKMK KMNM**
Intermediate Form	***Ne NiNeNeNe NeNe***

Sentences

நாம் அரங்கத்துக்கு வந்தோம்

References

Ananth Ramakrishnan, Sankar Kuppan, and Sobha Lalitha Devi. 2009. *Automatic Generation of Tamil Lyrics for Melodies*. Proceedings of the Workshop on Computational Approaches to Linguistic Creativity, CALC'09, Boulder, Colorado:40-46.

Arulmozhi P, Sobha. L. 2006. *Semantic Tagging for Language Processing*. 34th All India conference for Dravidian Linguistics (June 22-24, 2006), Trivandrum, India.

Bala Sundara Raman L, Ishwar S, and Sanjeeth Kumar Ravindranath. 2003. *Context Free Grammar for Natural Language Constructs – An implementation for Venpa Class of Tamil Poetry*. 6th International Tamil Internet Conference and Exhibition, Tamil Internet 2003 (August 22-24, 2003), Chennai, India.

Guido Gonzato. 2003. *The ABCPlus Project* http://abcplus.sourceforge.net.

Hisar Maruli Manurung. 2004. *An evolutionary approach to poetry generation*. Ph.D. Thesis, University of Edinburg.

Menaka S, Vijay Sundar Ram, and Sobha Lalitha Devi. 2010. *Morphological Generator for Tamil*. Proceedings of the Knowledge Sharing event on Morphological Analysers and Generators (March 22-23, 2010), LDC-IL, Mysore, India:82-96.

Rajam V.S. 1992. *A Reference Grammar of Classical Tamil Poetry (150 B.C.-pre-5th/6th century A.D.)*. Memoirs of the American Philosophical Society, Philadelphia: 113-240.

Tholkaappiyar. 5th Century B.C. *Tholkaapiyam - http://www.tamil.net/projectmadurai/pub/pm0100/tolkap.pdf*.

Representing Story Plans in SUMO

Jeffrey Cua
Center for Human Language Technologies
De La Salle University, Manila, Philippines
cuajeffreyleonardcompro1@yahoo.com

Ethel Ong
College of Computer Studies
De La Salle University, Manila, Philippines
ethel.ong@delasalle.ph

Ruli Manurung
Faculty of Computer Science
University of Indonesia, Jakarta, Indonesia
maruli@cs.ui.ac.id

Adam Pease
Articulate Software
Angwin, California, USA
apease@articulatesoftware.com

Abstract

Automatic story generation systems require a body of commonsense knowledge about the basic relationships between concepts we find everyday in our world in order to produce interesting narratives that describe human actions and world events. This paper presents an ongoing work that investigates the use of Suggested Upper Merged Ontology (SUMO) to represent storytelling knowledge and its inference engine Sigma to query actions and events that may take place in the story to be generated. The resulting story plan (*fabula*) is also represented in SUMO, allowing for a single story representation to be realized in various human languages.

1 Introduction

People combine words and events from their knowledge source of words, their meanings and their relationships in order to tell stories about their lives, their communities, and their daily experiences. In order for computers to achieve the same level of expressiveness to provide a more fluent man-machine interaction, they must be provided with the same collection of knowledge about the basic relationships between things and events.

Picture Books (Solis et al, 2009), an automatic story generator that generates story text for children from a given input set of picture elements (backgrounds, characters and objects), utilized a semantic ontology whose design has been adapted from ConceptNet (Liu and Singh, 2004). The background serves as the setting of the story and is also used to determine the theme. Semantic concepts needed by the story planner, specifically objects, story events, and character actions are classified according to the semantic categories of ConceptNet, namely things, spatial, events, actions, and functions. This mapping approach constrained the flexibility of the system, as new themes would entail repopulating the sequences of possible events manually into the knowledge base. Events and actions are selected according to their associated themes, and not marked with preconditions that specify constraints under which certain actions can be performed and the corresponding consequential events that may arise.

Swartjes (2006) developed a story world ontology containing two layers, the upper story world ontology and the domain-specific world ontology. The upper story world ontology is independent of any story structures or story domains and models a vast amount of possible actions and events. It is also limited to high-level concepts that are meta, generic or abstract to address a broad range of domain areas. A domain-specific story world ontology, on the other hand, applies the upper story world ontology to a certain story domain.

Kooijman (2004) suggests the use of the Suggested Upper Merged Ontology (SUMO) as an upper ontology to capture the semantics of world knowledge. SUMO (Niles and Pease, 2001) is an

Proceedings of the NAACL HLT 2010 Second Workshop on Computational Approaches to Linguistic Creativity, pages 40–48,
Los Angeles, California, June 2010.

open source formal and public ontology. It is a collection of well-defined and well-documented concepts, interconnected into a logical theory. It numbers some 20,000 terms and 70,000 axioms. Axioms are in first-order logic form (with some higher order extensions) and reflect commonsense notions that are generally recognized among the concepts. They place a constraint on the interpretation of concepts and provide guidelines for automated reasoning systems such as Sigma (Pease, 2003). Formal terms in SUMO are mapped to synsets in WordNet (Pease, 2006).

There are other noteworthy ontologies that can be considered. Like SUMO, Cyc (Lenat, 1995) is a large-scale, language-independent and extensible knowledge base and commonsense reasoning engine, but it is proprietary and its open-source version, OpenCyc[1], has no inference rules. DOLCE (Gangemi, 2003) is a small-scale descriptive ontology with a cognitive orientation. BFO (Smith, 1998) is another small-scale upper ontology supporting domain ontologies developed for scientific research domain, such as biomedicine. Thus, no ontology other than SUMO had the characteristics of being comprehensive enough to include formalizations that represent detailed elements of everyday life (e.g., *furniture*, *breaking an object*, *emotion*), being open-source, having expressiveness of at least first order predicate calculus so that arbitrary rules about actions and consequences can be represented, having an associated open-source first-order inference engine, and a language generation capability so that stories can be automatically presented in multiple human languages

This paper presents SUMOs (SUMO Stories), an automatic story generator that uses first-order logic to declaratively describe models of the world, specifically those aspects of the world that represent storytelling knowledge for children's stories of the fable form. The story planner then utilizes an open source browsing and inference engine Sigma to infer this knowledge to generate a story plan (*fabula*) also in first-order logic form.

Using first-order logic enables a less restricted semantics compared to description logic, which is commonly used for knowledge representation of large ontologies. Though having lesser constraints will have an impact on the speed of inference, it is overcome by the advantage of having greater representational capability. In particular, the axiomatic nature of actions and their consequences, so essential for reasoning about narrative structures, is not supported by description logics, which focus on category and instance membership reasoning.

Section 2 provides a background on the knowledge required by story generation and how these were represented in Picture Books, which is used as the basis for the storytelling knowledge. Section 3 discusses the representation of the storytelling knowledge to SUMO. The SUMOs architecture depicting the interaction between the story planner and Sigma to derive the story plan is then presented in Section 4. The paper concludes with a summary of what we have accomplished so far, and presents further work that can be done.

2 Storytelling Knowledge

Theune and her colleagues (2006) presented five levels of the different aspects of a story that must be represented in the semantic network. These are the story world knowledge, character representations, a causal and temporal network to represent plot structures, representational model of narratological concepts, and the representation of the story's potential effects on the user. Only the first four levels are included in this study.

According to Swartjes (2006), a story is composed of a story world where the story takes place, the characters that interact in the story world, and the associated objects. Consider the story generated by Picture Books in Table 1 about *Rizzy the rabbit* who learns to be honest (Hong et al, 2008).

The afternoon was windy. Rizzy the rabbit was in the dining room. She played near a lamp. Rizzy broke the lamp. She was scared. Mommy Francine saw that the lamp was broken. Rizzy told Mommy Francine that Daniel broke the lamp. Daniel the dog told her that he did not break the lamp. Daniel was upset. He got punished. Mommy Francine told Daniel that he was grounded. He cried. Rizzy felt guilty. She told Mommy Francine that she broke the lamp. Mommy Francine told Rizzy that she should have been honest. Rizzy apologized to Mommy Francine. Mommy Francine forgave Rizzy. Rizzy apologized to Daniel. He forgave her. Mommy Francine told Rizzy to be honest. She told her that being honest is good. From that day onwards, Rizzy always was honest.

Table 1. Sample story generated by Picture Books (Hong et al, 2008)

[1] OpenCyc web site, http://www.opencyc.org/

The story elements in Table 1 were determined from the background (i.e., *dining room*), the characters (i.e., *Rizzy and her mommy Francine*) and object (i.e., *lamp*) that the child user places into his/her picture using the Picture Editor of the system in Figure 1.

The background serves as the main setting of the story, and combined with the selected objects, is used to determine the theme. Consider the *bedroom* setting. If the associated object is a *lamp*, then the theme is about bravery (i.e., *do not be afraid of the dark*). If the object is a set of *toy blocks*, the theme can be about being neat. In Picture Books, such associations are manually determined and entered into the database. In SUMOs, these associations should be inferred automatically through axioms that should be commonsense, and not be explicit encoding of narrative knowledge.

Figure 2. Picture Editor (Hong et al, 2008)

Stories generated by Picture Books follow a basic plot dictated by Machado (2003) that flows from negative to positive and comprises four subplots, namely the problem, rising action, solution and climax. The theme is subdivided into these four subplots, each representing a major event in the story.

Each subplot contains at least two author goals representing the goal of the scene and the corresponding consequence of the goal. An author goal is translated into one or more character goals, each representing an action performed by the character (main, secondary, or adult character) in order to achieve the author goal. A character goal translates directly to one declarative sentence in the generated story. Table 2 shows the author goals and the character goals for some of the sentences in the story in Table 1.

The design of the character goal is based from the action operators of Uijlings (2006) which is easily transformed to a declarative sentence in active voice using the surface realizer *simpleNLG* (Venour and Reiter, 2008). In the case of Picture Books, however, the approach resulted in a story where every sentence describes an action or a feeling (i.e., *scared*, *guilty*, *upset*) that is performed by the character, as seen in Table 1.

Subplot #1	
Author goal 1.1:	
Goal of the scene	Child is doing an activity
Character goal	*<character> plays <object>*
Resulting text	*Rizzy the rabbit played near a lamp.*
Author goal 1.2:	
Goal consequence	Child caused a problem
Character goal	*<character> destroys <object>*
Resulting text	*Rizzy broke the lamp.*
Subplot #2	
Author goal 2.1:	
Goal of the scene	Child lied
Character goal	*<main character> told <adult character> that <secondary character> <did the action>*
Resulting text	*Rizzy told Mommy Francine that Daniel the dog broke the lamp.*
Author goal 2.2:	
Goal consequence	Another child gets punished
Character goal #1	*<secondary character> receives <punishment>*
Resulting text #1	*Daniel the dog got punished.*
Character goal #2	*<adult character> issues <punishment> to <secondary character>*
Resulting text #2	*Mommy Francine told Daniel that he was grounded.*

Table 2. Sample author goals and character goals associated with the theme *Being Honest* (Hong et al, 2008)

The story planner of Picture Books utilizes two types of knowledge, the operational knowledge and the domain knowledge. The operational knowledge contains a static description of the different backgrounds and their associated themes and objects, the child characters and their corresponding parent characters, as well as the occupation of the parents. For each theme, the set of character goals needed to instantiate the major events in the theme are also specified.

The domain knowledge, on the other hand, contains a semantic description of objects and events that can occur, as well as actions that can be performed. For example, *breaking an object* results to *getting punished*, and *grounded* is a form of *punishment*.

Character goals are instantiated by accessing the semantic ontology to search for concepts that are directly related to the input concept. There are two search methods. The first method searches for another concept that has a relationship with the given concept while satisfying the semantic category. For example, ontoSpatial("play") triggers a search for all concepts connected to *play* within the *spatial* semantic category, such as the semantic relationship locationOf("play", "park"). The second method searches for a path that semantically relates the two given concepts. For example, ontoAction("vase", "method of destruction") triggers a search for a path to relate how a *vase* can be destroyed, and yields the following relationships:

```
CapableOf("break", "vase")
Isa("method of destruction", "break")
```

3 Representing Storytelling Knowledge in SUMO

A crucial part of the work involved in the development of SUMOs is the representation of the storytelling knowledge and the evolving story plan in SUMO and the use of the Sigma reasoning engine to infer story facts and events.

The storytelling knowledge represented in SUMO includes the semantic description about concepts, objects and their relationships. From a given input set of story elements comprising the selected background, characters, and objects, a query is sent to Sigma to determine a possible starting action that can be performed by the main character in the story. The story then progresses based on the relationships of character actions and reactions, which are the stored facts in SUMO.

Similar to Picture Books, the resulting story plan is created based on a pre-authored plot of problem, rising action, resolution and climax. But instead of attaching the next set of actions and emotions of characters to author goals, in SUMOs, the set of actions that a character can do – reaction to events and objects, experience emotions such as joy and sadness, and subsequent actions based on their emotions – are represented in SUMO logic.

The storytelling knowledge was formulated using a set of predicates that can be classified into four main types. Factual predicates specify properties of characters, objects, and locations. Semantic predicates define the semantic relationships between concepts. Actions and events predicates define the causal relationships between actions and events. Thematic predicates represent a new set of predicates to relate story themes to actions.

3.1 Conceptualizing Story Characters, Objects, and Backgrounds

Factual predicates represent the characters, their roles, the locations, and the objects that may comprise a story. The *class* and *subclass* axioms of SUMO[2] are used to define the set of characters, objects and locations.

Children's stories of the fable form are portrayed by animals that can capture the imagination and attention of the readers. Animal characters are given names, such as *Ellen the elephant*, *Rizzy the rabbit*, and *Leo the lion*, to give the impression that the characters are friends that the children are getting to know better through reading the story (Solis et al, 2009). Representing this in SUMO entails the use of the *subclass* axiom to represent class inheritance as shown below:

```
(subclass RabbitCharacter StoryCharacter)
```

Class definitions include slots that describe the attributes of instances of the class and their relations to other instances (Noy, 2001). A character in SUMOs has the attributes *type* (whether adult or child), *gender*, and *name*. An example axiom to represent a female child *RabbitCharacter* whose name will be "*Rizzy*" is shown below. Similar axioms are defined for all the other characters.

```
(=>
   (and
    (instance ?RABBIT RabbitCharacter)
    (attribute ?RABBIT Female)
    (attribute ?RABBIT Child))
   (name ?RABBIT "Rizzy"))
```

Backgrounds and objects are also defined using the *subclass* axiom and inherit from existing classes in SUMO, for example,

[2] SUMO Ontology Portal, http://www.ontologyportal.org/

```
(subclass LivingRoom Room)
(subclass Lamp LightFixture)
(subclass Lamp ElectricDevice)
(attribute Lamp Fragile)
```

Further definitions can be provided for *living room* to differentiate it from other rooms, such as being disjoint from bathroom, and has a primary purpose of supporting social interaction, as shown below. Similarly, the definition for *lamp* can also be extended to distinguish it from other electric light fixtures, e.g., a lamp is moveable unlike a chandelier, but is plugged in when operating unlike a flashlight.

```
(=>
   (instance ?R LivingRoom)
   (hasPurpose ?R
        (exists (?S)
          (and
             (instance ?S SocialInteraction)
             (located ?S ?R)))))
(disjoint LivingRoom Bathroom)
```

3.2 Representing Semantic Concepts

Aside from the properties of objects that are modeled using the *attribute* axiom, semantic relationships that may hold between two concepts involving types of activities or actions, character emotions, locations of objects, and abilities of characters or objects must also be modeled. Table 3 shows sample semantic relationships for these concepts as represented in Picture Books, following the semantic categories of ConceptNet (Liu and Singh, 2004).

Objects	IsA (doll, toys)
Activities	IsA (play games, activity)
Concepts	IsA (grounded, punishment) IsA (disorder, problem) IsA (no appetite, problem) IsA (dizzy, discomfort) IsA (itchy, discomfort)
Emotions	IsA (happy, emotion) IsA (scared, emotion)
Reaction to Events	EffectOf (break object, scared) EffectOf (meet new friends, smile)
Location	LocationOf (toys, toy store)
Capability	CapableOf (lamp, break) CapableOf (glass of water, break) CanBe (toys, scattered)

Table 3. Semantic relationships in Picture Books based on ConceptNet (Hong et al, 2008)

In SUMOs, all *isA(entity1, entity2)* relations were replaced with the axiom *(subclass entity1 entity2)*. To specify that an entity is in a location, i.e., *locationOf(toys, toy store)*, first, we create an instance of a *toystore* and then specify that a certain *toy* instance is in that *toystore*, as follows:

```
(=>
  (instance ?TOYSTORE ToyStore)
  (exists (?TOY)
    (and
      (instance ?TOY Toy)
      (located ?TOY ?TOYSTORE))))
```

The *capability* axiom is used to conceptualize the capability relation *(capability ?process ?role ?obj)*. It specifies that *?obj* has the specified *?role* in the *?process*. For example, a *lamp* or a *glass* is the patient (receiver) of the process *breaking*, while a *toy* is the patient for the process *scattering*.

```
(capability Breaking experiencer Lamp)
(capability Breaking experiencer Glass)
(capability Scattering experiencer Toy)
```

Reaction to events is expressed using the *if-else* axiom of SUMO, for example, if a child character causes an accident (a damage), then he/she will feel anxiety. Emotions are represented using the *attribute* relation.

```
(=>
  (and
   (instance ?ACCIDENT Damaging)
   (instance ?CHARACTER StoryCharacter)
   (attribute ?CHARACTER Child)
   (agent ?ACCIDENT ?CHARACTER))
  ((attribute ?CHARACTER Anxiety)))
```

3.3 Conceptualizing Actions and Events

Swartjes (2006) noted that organizing actions and events, and causally relating them, is an essential step in story generation. Independent of the story plot, the causes and effects of character actions can be used to describe the events that form the story.

Actions define activities that can be performed by a character in the story, such as *play*, *tell a lie*, or *cry*. Events, on the other hand, occur in the story as a result of performing some actions, such as a *lamp breaking* as a result of a character or an object hitting it. Swartjes (2006) further notes that events are not executed by a character.

Action predicates are used to define the actions that may take place given a set of world state. Consider the axiom below which provides a set of four possible actions – *RecreationOrExercise*, *Looking*, *Maintaining*, and *Poking* – that can be performed (as an agent) or experienced by a child character who is situated *near* a *lamp* object in the story world. These four actions are subclasses of the *IntentionalProcess* of SUMO.

```
(=>
 (and
  (orientation ?CHARACTER ?OBJECT Near)
  (instance ?CHARACTER StoryCharacter)
  (attribute ?CHARACTER Child)
  (instance ?OBJECT Lamp))
 (and
  (capability RecreationOrExercise
                    experiencer ?CHARACTER)
  (capability Looking experiencer ?CHARACTER)
  (capability Maintaining experiencer ?CHARACTER)
  (capability Poking experiencer ?CHARACTER)))
```

Again, the *capability* relation is used but in this instance, to specify that the character has the role of experiencing the specified process. While both the agent and the experiencer roles represent the doer of a process, an experiencer does not entail a causal relation between its arguments.

Event predicates are used to model explicit events that may take place as a result of some character actions. Consider again the *exists* axiom below which states that an instance of an event (in this case *damaging*) can occur when there is a child character (the *agent*) playing near a fragile object. The *subprocess* axiom is used to represent a temporally distinguished part of a process and also expresses a chain of cause and effect subprocesses for *playing* and *damaging*. The recipient (*patient*) of the event is the object.

```
(=>
 (and
  (agent ?X ?CHARACTER)
  (instance ?CHARACTER StoryCharacter)
  (attribute ?CHARACTER Child)
  (instance ?OBJECT Object)
  (attribute ?OBJECT Fragile)
  (instance ?X RecreationOrExercise)
  (orientation ?CHARACTER ?OBJECT Near)
 (exists (?DAMAGE)
  (and
   (instance ?DAMAGE Damaging)
   (subProcess ?DAMAGE ?X)
   (agent ?DAMAGE ?CHARACTER)
   (patient ?DAMAGE ?OBJECT))))
```

Although suitable for inference, the given axiom does not fully capture the desired truth as the notion of time is not represented. The axiom says "*if a child plays at any point in time, and is near an object at any point in time (not necessarily while playing), then the object gets damaged during playing*". The more accurate axiom below uses *holdsDuring* to show that the time frames of the actual playing and being near the object are the same, thus increasing the likelihood of the character who is playing to cause the damage.

```
(=>
 (and
  (instance ?X RecreationOrExercise)
  (agent ?X ?CHARACTER)
  (instance ?CHARACTER StoryCharacter)
  (attribute ?CHARACTER Child)
  (instance ?OBJECT Object)
  (attribute ?OBJECT Fragile)
  (holdsDuring (WhenFn ?X)
     (orientation ?CHARACTER ?OBJECT Near))
 (exists (?DAMAGE)
  (and
   (instance ?DAMAGE Damaging)
   (subProcess ?DAMAGE ?X)
   (agent ?DAMAGE ?CHARACTER)
   (patient ?DAMAGE ?OBJECT))))
```

As the representation shows, SUMO is quite capable of encoding temporal properties of events with its temporal qualification. However, inferencing with rules involving time relations between events is currently not supported by Sigma (Corda et al, 2008). Nevertheless, efforts are underway to perform true higher-order logical inference (Sutcliffe et al, 2009).

The next step involves deriving axioms to represent the different ways in which an object can be damaged depending on its attribute, for example, fragile objects can break while paper-based objects such as books and paintings can be torn. Consideration must also be made to determine if a damage is an accident or intentional.

3.4 Conceptualizing Story Themes

Themes can also be mapped to SUMO as thematic predicates, and the story planner can identify a theme either based on the first action that was performed, or based on user selection. In the latter case, when Sigma returns all possible actions, the planner can choose one based on the theme.

4 System Architecture

The architecture of SUMOs, shown in Figure 2, has two main modules, the Story Editor and the Story Planner, both of which interact with Sigma[3] to retrieve story facts from the SUMO ontology as well as to assert new axioms representing the developing story plan back to SUMO.

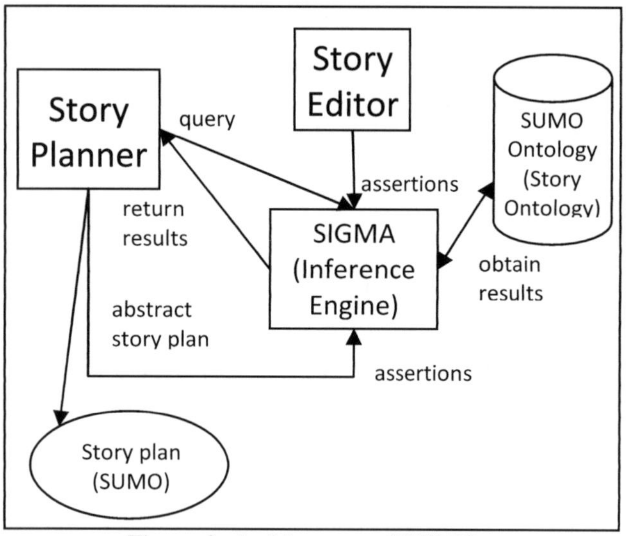

Figure 2. Architecture of SUMOs

The Story Editor handles the generation of assertions corresponding to the input picture elements specified by the user.

The Story Planner is responsible for planning the flow of events in the story. It uses a meta-knowledge about children's story comprising of five phases – introduction, problem, rising action, solution, and climax. The planner determines and phrases the queries that are sent to Sigma and generates additional axioms based on the query results in order to expand the story plan. The generated axioms are asserted back to Sigma for inclusion in the SUMO ontology to be used again for further inferencing.

Queries sent to Sigma can be classified into three categories. Concept-based queries concern classes and instances, and are used to determine direct and indirect subclass and class-instance relationships while relation-based queries infer knowledge by considering transitivity, symmetry and inversion of relations (Corda et al, 2008). Action-based queries identify a set of actions based on the current world state to drive the story. A fourth category, time-event queries, currently not supported by Sigma, should reason about temporal and event-based specifications.

The interaction between the Story Planner and Sigma in Figure 2 raises an issue of search control. In Picture Books and SUMOs, information that guides the story planning can be *bottom-up*, i.e. the actions and events are determined based on what is possible within the story ontology, e.g. through the various capability axioms, or *top-down*, i.e. actions are selected based on Machado's narrative subplot knowledge. Currently, the Story Planner is responsible for managing the process. However, if both these sources of knowledge and constraints can be represented in first-order logic, the search control of the story planning process can be recast as a theorem proving task, i.e. one that searches for a proof that satisfies all constraints. This is a future research direction.

The following section presents a more detailed trace of system operation and the contents of a story plan in first-order logic.

4.1 Generating Story Plans

The first part of the story plan contains assertions to represent the initial elements of the story. Using the story in Table 1 as an example, lines 1 to 6 below assert the main child character and her parent, while lines 7 to 8 assert the background and the object, respectively.

```
1>  (instance Rabbit1 RabbitCharacter)
2>  (attribute Rabbit1 Child)
3>  (attribute Rabbit1 Female)
4>  (instance Rabbit2 RabbitCharacter)
5>  (attribute Rabbit2 Adult)
6>  (attribute Rabbit2 Female)
7>  (instance LivingRoom1 LivingRoom)
8>  (instance Lamp1 Lamp)
```

The next step involves initializing the locations of these story elements. Currently, it is setup that all objects would be situated in the background and the first child character would always be near the first object, as shown in the assertions below.

```
9>  (located Rabbit1 LivingRoom1)
10> (located Lamp1 LivingRoom1)
11> (orientation Rabbit1 Lamp1 Near)
```

This, however, creates the assumption that the child character is already in the location near objects which he will interact with, which may not

[3] Sigma Knowledge Engineering Environment, http://sigmakee.sourceforge.net

necessarily be true and reduces the flexibility of the system. In order to create more varied stories, the initial location can be identified based on the theme and the first event that the user would want to likely happen in the story.

From the initial set of assertions, the story planner issues its first concept-based query to Sigma with "(name Rabbit1 ?X)" to determine a name for the main character, *Rabbit1*, and receives *"Rizzy"* as a result. This is asserted to the story plan as:

12> (name Rabbit1 "Rizzy")

The next query is the first action-based query used to determine the first action to start the story flow. Given "(capability ?X experiencer Rabbit1)", which is intended for identifying the set of possible starting actions that the main character, *Rabbit1*, can perform with the object in the background, Sigma returns the following list (assuming the story facts given in the previous section):

X = [RecreationOrExercise, Looking,
Maintaining, Poking]

Assuming the planner selects *RecreationOrExercise*, the following assertions are then added to the story plan:

13> (instance RecOrEx1 RecreationOrExercise)
14> (agent RecOrEx1 Rabbit1)

At this point, the introduction phase of the story plan has been completed. The problem phase begins with a query to identify any instances of problems that can occur, i.e. "(instance ?X Damaging)". Damaging the object *lamp* causes its attribute to be changed, and again we query Sigma for this change of state with "(attribute Lamp1 ?X)" yielding the result *broken*, and the corresponding emotional state of the character "(attribute Rabbit1 ?X)". The following assertions were added to the plan:

15> (instance (sk0 Rabbit1 Lamp1
RecOrEx1) Damaging)
16> (attribute Lamp1 Broken)
17> (attribute Rabbit1 Anxiety)

While a full explanation of skolemization is not possible here for space reasons, we note that the second argument of assertion #15 (derived from Sigma's answer to the query) stands for the existence of an unnamed term, in this case, that there is an instance of a *Damaging* process. The agent (*Rabbit1*), patient (*Lamp1*), and the action (*RecOrEx1*) that caused the problem were all provided in the query result.

4.2 Generating Surface Text

SUMO-based story plans provide a form of *interlingua* where story details are represented in logical form. The logical representation allows generation of the same story in different languages (that are connected to WordNet). Sigma already has a language generator, with templates for English, and an initial set for Tagalog (Borra et al, 2010). Work is currently underway to enhance the existing language generator in Sigma and make the generated text more natural. Sigma can then be used to generate stories automatically from the knowledge asserted in the story generation process.

5 Conclusions and Further Work

The paper presented a preliminary work aimed at representing storytelling knowledge in SUMO and using Sigma as inference engine to assist the planner in generating story plans. Further work focuses on modeling the emotional state of the character as a result of some event (e.g., feeling worried, guilty or scared due to causing some problems in the world state), changes in character traits as the story progresses (e.g., from negative trait to positive trait as the story flows from rule violation to value acquisition), and enhancing the representation for story themes. Once a set of knowledge has been developed, these should be evaluated systematically through validation of the rules for logical consistency with the theorem prover. A future goal is to apply the metrics proposed by Callaway & Lester (2002) in StoryBook to evaluate with actual users if the generated stories are better and more varied as compared to that of Picture Books.

Although SUMO is quite capable of representing time and sequences, reasoning with temporally qualified expression is challenging for any theorem prover. The works of (Sutcliffe et al, 2009) to extend the inference engine to handle reasoning over temporal relations should be explored further to allow SUMOs to generate story plans that consider temporal relations between actions and events.

Finally, story generators will benefit its readers if the generated stories are narrated orally. SUMOs can be explored further to model various emotions to provide annotations in the surface story text which will then be fed to a text to speech tool for speech generation.

References

Borra, A., Pease, A., Roxas, R. and Dita, S. 2010. Introducing Filipino WordNet. In: *Principles, Construction and Application of Multilingual Wordnets: Proceedings of the 5th Global WordNet Conference*, Mumbai, India.

Callaway, C. B., and Lester, J. C. 2002. Narrative Prose Generation. *Artificial Intelligence*, 139(2):213-252, Elsevier Science Publishers Ltd., Essex, UK.

Corda, I., Bennett, B., and Dimitrova, V. 2008. Interacting with an Ontology to Explore Historical Domains. *Proceedings of the 2008 First International Workshop on Ontologies in Interactive Systems*, 65-74, IEEE Computer Society.

Gangemi, A., Guarino, N., Masolo, C., and Oltramari, A. 2003. *AI Magazine*, 24(3):13-24, Association for the Advancement of Artificial Intelligence.

Kooijman, R. 2004. De virtuele verhalenverteller: voorstel voor het gebruik van een upper-ontology en een nieuwe architectuur. *Technical Report*. University of Twente, Department of Electrical Engineering, Mathematics and Computer Science.

Hong, A., Solis, C., Siy, J.T., and Tabirao, E. 2008. *Picture Books: Automated Story Generator*. Undergraduate Thesis, De La Salle University, Manila, Philippines.

Lenat, D.B. 1995. Cyc: A Large-Scale Investment in Knowledge Infrastructure, *Communications of the ACM*, 38(11).

Liu, H. and Singh, P. 2004. Commonsense Reasoning in and over Natural Language. *Proceedings of the 8th International Conference on Knowledge-Based Intelligent Information and Engineering Systems*, 293-306, Wellington, New Zealand, Springer Berlin.

Machado, J. 2003. Storytelling. In *Early Childhood Experiences in Language Arts: Emerging Literacy*, 304-319. Clifton Park, N.Y., Thomson/Delmar Learning.

Niles, I. and Pease, A. 2001. Towards A Standard Upper Ontology. *Proceedings of Formal Ontology in Information Systems* (FOIS 2001), 2-9, October 17-19, Ogunquit, Maine, USA.

Noy, N. and McGuinness, D. 2001. Ontology Development 101: A Guide to Creating Your First Ontology. *Stanford Knowledge Systems Laboratory Technical Report KSL-01-05* and *Stanford Medical Informatics Technical Report SMI-2001-0880*, March 2001.

Ong, E. 2009. Prospects in Creative Natural Language Processing. *Proceedings of the 6th National Natural Language Processing Research Symposium*, De La Salle University, Manila, Philippines.

Pease, A. 2006. Formal Representation of Concepts: The Suggested Upper Merged Ontology and Its Use in Linguistics. *Ontolinguistics. How Ontological Status Shapes the Linguistic Coding of Concepts*. Schalley, A.C. and Zaefferer, D. (ed.), Vorbereitung Berlin, New York.

Pease, A. 2003. The Sigma Ontology Development Environment. *Working Notes of the IJCAI-2003 Workshop on Ontology and Distributed Systems*, vol. 71 of CEUR Workshop Proceeding series.

Riedl, M. and Young, R.M. 2004. An Intent-Driven Planner for Multi-Agent Story Generation. *Proceedings of the Third International Joint Conference on Autonomous Agents and Multi-Agent Systems*, 186-193, Washington DC, USA, IEEE Computer Society.

Smith, B. 1998. The Basic Tools of Formal Ontology. *Formal Ontology in Information Systems*, Nicola Guarino (ed), IOS Press, Washington. *Frontiers in Artificial Intelligence and Applications*, 19-28.

Solis, C., Siy, J.T., Tabirao, E., and Ong, E. 2009. Planning Author and Character Goals for Story Generation. *Proceedings of the NAACL Human Language Technology 2009 Workshop on Computational Approaches to Linguistic Creativity*, 63-70, Boulder, Colorado, USA.

Sutcliffe, G., Benzmüller, C., Brown, C.E., and Theiss, F. 2009. Progress in the Development of Automated Theorem Proving for Higher-order Logic. *Automated Deduction, 22nd International Conference on Automated Deduction*, Montreal, Canada, August 2-7, 2009. *Proceedings of the Lecture Notes in AI*, vol. 5663, 116-130, 2009, Springer.

Swartjes, I. 2006. *The Plot Thickens: Bringing Structure and Meaning into Automated Story Generation*. Master's Thesis, University of Twente, The Netherlands.

Theune, M., Nijholt, A., Oinonen, K., and Uijlings J. 2006. Designing a Story Database for Use in Automatic Story Generation. *Proceedings 5th International Conference Entertainment Computing*, Cambridge, UK. Lecturer Notes in Computer Science, 4161:298-301, Heidelberg, Springer Berlin.

Uijlings, J.R.R. 2006. *Designing a Virtual Environment for Story Generation*. MS Thesis, University of Amsterdam, The Netherlands.

Venour, C. and Reiter, E. 2008. *A Tutorial for Simplenlg*. http://www.csd.abdn.ac.uk/~ereiter/simplenlg

WordNet. 2006. *WordNet: A Lexical Database for the English Language*. Princeton University, New Jersey.

Computational Creativity Tools for Songwriters

Burr Settles
Machine Learning Department
Carnegie Mellon University
Pittsburgh, PA 15213 USA
bsettles@cs.cmu.edu

Abstract

This paper describes two natural language processing systems designed to assist songwriters in obtaining and developing ideas for their craft. *Titular* is a text synthesis algorithm for automatically generating novel song titles, which lyricists can use to back-form concepts and narrative story arcs. *LyriCloud* is a word-level language "browser" or "explorer," which allows users to interactively select words and receive lyrical suggestions in return. Two criteria for creativity tools are also presented along with examples of how they guided the development of these systems, which were used by musicians during an international songwriting contest.

1 Introduction

Writing lyrics for popular music is challenging. Even apart from musical considerations, well-crafted lyrics should succinctly tell a story, express emotion, or create an image in the listener's mind with vivid and original language. Finding the right words, from an evocative title to a refrain, hook, or narrative detail, is often difficult even for full-time professional songwriters.

This paper considers the task of creating "intelligent" interactive lyric-writing tools for musicians. As a preliminary case study, I discuss two systems that (1) suggest novel song titles and (2) find interesting words given a seed word as input, and deployed them online for participants in an international songwriting event called FAWM[1] (February Album Writing Month). The goal of this event—which attracts both professional and amateur musicians worldwide—is to compose 14 new works of music (roughly an album's worth) during the month of February. Working at a rate of one new song every two days on average is taxing, described by some participants as a "musical marathon." To maintain pace, songwriters are constantly looking for new ideas, which makes them good candidates for using computational creativity tools. Typical lyric-writing tools consist of rhyme or phrase dictionaries which are searchable but otherwise static, passive resources. By contrast, we wish to develop advanced software which uses learned linguistic knowledge to actively help stimulate creative thought.

To formalize the task of developing computational creativity tools, let us first define *creativity* as "the ability to extrapolate beyond existing ideas, rules, patterns, interpretations, etc., and to generate meaningful new ones." By this working definition, which is similar to Zhu et al. (2009), tools that assist humans in creative endeavors should:

1. Suggest instances *unlike* the majority that exist. If one were to model instances statistically, system proposals should be "outliers."

2. Suggest instances that are *meaningful*. Purely random proposals might be outliers, but they are not likely to be interesting or useful.

Previous approaches to linguistic lyric-modeling have generally not focused on creativity, but rather on quantifying "hit potential" (Yang et al., 2007), which is arguably the opposite, or classifying musical genre (Li and Ogihara, 2004; Neumayer and

[1] http://fawm.org

Proceedings of the NAACL HLT 2010 Second Workshop on Computational Approaches to Linguistic Creativity, pages 49–57,
Los Angeles, California, June 2010.

Rauber, 2007). There has been some work on automatically generating percussive lyrics to accompany a given piece of musical input (Oliveira et al., 2007; Ramakrishnan et al., 2009), and there exists a rich body of related work on natural language generation for fiction (Montfort, 2006; Solis et al., 2009), poetry (Gervás, 2001; Manurung, 2004; Netzer et al., 2009), and even jokes (Binstead, 1996). However, the goal of these systems is to be an "artificial artist" which can create complete works of language autonomously, rather than interactive tools for assisting humans in their creative process.

A few computational lyric-writing tools have been developed outside of academia, such as *Verbasizer*, which was famously co-created by rock star David Bowie to help him brainstorm ideas (Thompson, 2007). These types of systems take a small amount of seed text as input, such as a newspaper article, and generate novel phrases by iterating through random word permutations. However, these approaches fail the second criterion for creativity tools, since the majority of output is not meaningful. Many other so-called lyric generators exist on the Internet[2], but these are by and large "Mad-Lib" style fill-in-the-blanks meant for amusement rather than more serious artistic exploration.

The contribution of this work is to develop and study methods that satisfy both criteria for computational creativity tools—that their suggestions are both *unlikely* and *meaningful*—and to demonstrate that these methods are useful to humans in practice. To do this, I employ statistical natural language models induced from a large corpus of song lyrics to produce real-time interactive programs for exploring songwriting ideas. The rest of this paper is organized as follows. Section 2 describes the overall approach and implementation details for these tools. Section 3 presents some empirical and anecdotal system evaluations. Section 4 summarizes my findings, discusses limitations of the current tools, and proposes future directions for work in this vein.

2 Methodology

Davis (1992) describes the discipline of songwriting as a multi-step process, beginning with *activation* and *association*. Activation, according to Davis, involves becoming hyper-observant, embracing spontaneous ideas, and then choosing a title, theme, or progression around which to build a song. Association is the act of expanding on that initial theme or idea as much as possible. Subsequent steps are to develop, organize, and winnow down the ideas generated during the first two stages.

Following this philosophy, I decided to design two natural language processing systems aimed at stimulating songwriters during the early stages of the process, while adhering to the criteria for creativity tools defined in Section 1. I call these tools *Titular*, which suggests novel song titles as a starting point, and *LyriCloud*, which expands lyrical ideas by suggesting related words in the form of a "cloud."

To encourage songwriters to actually adopt these tools, they were deployed online as part of the official FAWM website for participants to use. This posed some development constraints, namely that the user interface be implemented in the PHP language and run in a shared web-hosting environment. Because of this setup, complex inference methods based on a large number of statistics had to be avoided in order to maintain speed and interactivity. Thus, I was limited to approaches where sufficient statistics could be pre-computed and stored in a database to be accessed quickly as needed.

To induce linguistic models for Titular and LyriCloud, existing song data were needed for training. For this, I used a "screen scraper" to extract song title, artist, and lyric fields from ubiquitous online lyrics websites. In this way, I collected a corpus of 137,787 songs by 15,940 unique artists. The collection spans multiple genres (e.g., pop/rock, hip-hop, R&B, punk, folk, blues, gospel, showtunes), and has good coverage of mainstream charting artists (e.g., Beyoncé, R.E.M., Van Halen) as well as more obscure independent performers (e.g., Over the Rhine, Dismemberment Plan). An estimated 85% of the songs are primarily in English.

2.1 Titular

Figure 1 shows example output from Titular, which presents the user with five suggested song titles at a time. Suggestions often combine visceral and contradictory images, like "Bleeding in the Laughter," while others lend themselves to more metaphorical interpretation, such as "Heads of Trick" (which

[2] http://www.song-lyrics-generator.org.uk

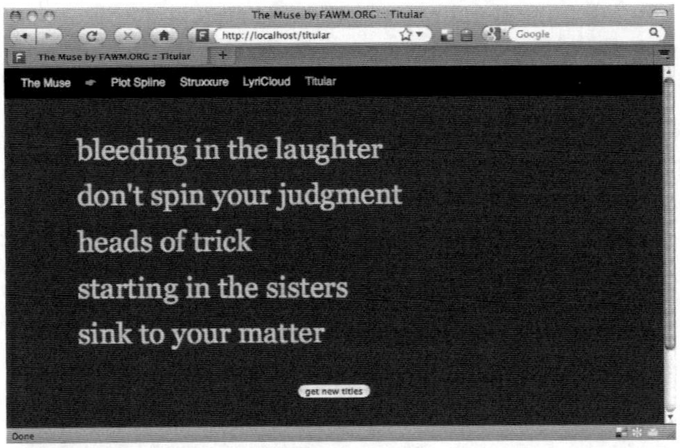

Figure 1: A screenshot of the Titular user interface.

Learned Template	Freq.	Example Source Title
JJ NN	3531	Irish Rover
VB	783	Breathe
VBN NN	351	Born Yesterday
NN and NN	205	Gin And Juice
NNP POS NN	167	Tom's Diner
FW NN	65	Voodoo Woman
VB and VB	57	Seek And Destroy
CD JJ NNS	49	99 Red Balloons
JJ , JJ NN	14	Bad, Bad Girl
you 're so JJ	8	You're So Vain
NN (the NN)	7	Silver (The Hunger)
VBG with a NN	4	Walking With A Zombie

Table 1: Example title templates induced by Titular.

evokes some sort of executive committee for deceit). Occasionally the output is syntactically valid, but a little too awkward to interpret sensibly, such as "Starting in the Sisters."

To accomplish this, I adopted a *template-based* approach (Deemter et al., 2005) to title synthesis. Instead of using hand-crafted templates, however, Titular learns its own using the following method:

1. Source titles in the training corpus are tokenized and tagged for part-of-speech (POS). Input is first lowercased to discourage the tagger from labeling everything NNP (proper noun).

2. The *open* word classes (i.e., various forms of adjectives, adverbs, nouns, and verbs) are substituted with their assigned POS tag, while *closed* words classes (i.e., conjunctions, determiners, prepositions, pronouns and punctuation) remain intact. Titular also remembers which words were substituted with which tag, in order to use them in generating new titles in the future. Vulgar and offensive words are filtered out using regular expressions.

3. The induced templates and words are culled if they occur in the corpus below a certain frequency. This step helps to counterbalance tagging errors, which is important because song titles are often too short to infer POS information accurately. Thresholds are set to 3 for templates and 2 for POS-word pairs.

Table 1 shows several example templates induced using this method. To generate new titles, Titular first randomly selects a template in proportion to its empirical frequency, and likewise selects words to replace each POS tag in the template (drawn from the set of words for the corresponding tag). This model can be thought of as a simple stochastic context-free grammar (Lari and Young, 1990) with only a small set of production rules. Specifically, the root nonterminal S goes to complete templates, e.g.,

$$S \rightarrow \text{VBG , VBG} \mid \text{UH , JJ NN !} \mid \ldots,$$

and POS nonterminals go to words that have been tagged accordingly in the corpus, e.g.,

$$\begin{aligned} \text{VBG} &\rightarrow \text{waiting} \mid \text{catching} \mid \text{going} \mid \ldots, \\ \text{JJ} &\rightarrow \text{good} \mid \text{little} \mid \text{sacrificial} \mid \ldots, \\ \text{NN} &\rightarrow \text{time} \mid \text{life} \mid \text{dream} \mid \ldots, \\ \text{UH} &\rightarrow \text{hey} \mid \text{oh} \mid \text{yeah} \mid \ldots, \end{aligned}$$

all with corresponding probabilities based on frequency. Using these production rules, Titular can generate novel titles like "Going, Waiting" or "Oh, Little Life!" The system learned 2,907 template production rules and 11,247 word production rules from the lyrics corpus, which were stored with frequency information in a MySQL database for deployment. Post-processing heuristics are implemented in the user interface to strip white-spaces from punctuation and contractions to improve readability. Output remains lowercased as an aesthetic decision.

An alternative approach to title generation is an n-gram model based on *Markov chains*, which are common for both natural language generation (Jurafsky and Martin, 2008) and music synthesis (Farbood and Schoner, 2001). For titles, each word w_i is generated with conditional probability

$P(w_i|w_{i-n}, \ldots, w_{i-1})$ based on the n words generated previously, using statistics gathered from titles in the lyrics corpus. However, this approach tends to simply recreate titles in the training data. In a preliminary study using $n = \{1, 2, 3, 4\}$ and 200 titles each, the proportion of suggestions that were verbatim recreations of existing titles ranged from 35% to 97%: . When n-gram titles do manage to be novel, they tend to be long and unintelligible, such as "Too Many A Woman First the Dark Clouds Will It Up" or "Born of Care 4 My Paradise." These two extremes satisfy one or the other, but not both of the criteria for creativity tools. By contrast, none of the 200 template-generated titles existed in the source database, and they tend to be more intelligible as well (see results in Section 3.1).

The template grammar offers several other advantages over the n-gram approach, including fewer inference steps (which results in fewer database queries) and helping to ensure that titles are well-formed with respect to longer-range syntactic dependencies (like matching parentheses). Constraining words by part-of-speech rather than immediate context also allows the system to create novel and unexpected word juxtapositions, which satisfies the first criterion for creativity tools, while remaining relatively coherent and meaningful, which helps satisfy the second criterion.

2.2 LyriCloud

Figure 2 shows example output from LyriCloud, which takes a *seed* (in this case, the word "dream" highlighted near the center) and suggests up to 25 related words arranged visually in a *cloud* (Bateman et al., 2008). The size of each word is intended to communicate its specificity to the cloud.

Notice that LyriCloud's notion of related words can be quite loose. Some suggestions are modifiers of the seed, like "broken dream" and "deep dream," although these invoke different senses of dream (metaphorical vs. literal). Some suggestions are part of an idiom involving the seed, such as "fulfill a dream," while others are synonyms/antonyms, or specializations/generalizations, such as "nightmare." Still other words might be useable as rhymes for the seed, like "smithereen" and even "thing" (loosely). The goal is to help the user see the seed word in a variety of senses and perspectives. Users

Figure 2: A screenshot of the LyriCloud user interface.

may also interact with the system by clicking with a pointer device on words in the cloud that they find interesting, and be presented with a new cloud based on the new seed. In this way, LyriCloud is a sort of "language browser" for lyrical ideas.

I liken the problem of generating interesting word clouds to an information retrieval task: given a seed word s, return a set of words that are related to s, with the constraint that they not be overly general terms. To do this, the corpus was pre-processed by filtering out common stop-words and words that occur in only one song, or fewer than five times in the entire corpus (this catches most typos and misspellings). As with Titular, vulgar and offensive words are filtered using regular expressions.

For a potential seed word s, we can compute a similarity score with every other word w in the corpus vocabulary using the following measure:

$$\mathrm{sim}(s, w) = \Big(1 + \log c(s, w)\Big) \cdot \log \frac{N}{u(w)},$$

where $c(s, w)$ is the number of times s and w co-occur in the same *line* of a lyric in the corpus, $u(w)$ is the number of unique words with which w occurs in any line of the corpus, and N is the size of the overall vocabulary. This is essentially the well-known log-tempered *tf·idf* measure from the information retrieval literature, if we treat each seed s as a "document" by concatenating all the lines of text in which s appears.

I also experimented with the co-occurence frequency $c(s, w)$ and *point-wise mutual information* (Church and Hanks, 1989) as similarity functions.

The former still used overly common words (e.g., "love," "heart," "baby"), which fails the first criterion for creativity tools, and the latter yielded overly seed-specific results (and often typos not filtered by the pre-processing step), which can fail the second criterion. The log-tempered *tf·idf* metric provided a reasonable balance between the two extremes.

To generate a new cloud from a given seed, up to 25 words are randomly sampled from the top 300 ranked by similarity, which are pre-computed and stored in the database for efficient lookup. The sampled words are then sorted alphabetically for display and scaled using a polynomial equation:

$$\text{size}(w) = f_0 + f_1 \cdot \left(1 - \frac{\text{rank}(w)}{K}\right)^4,$$

where f_0 and f_1 are constants that bound the minimum and maximum font size, and K is the number of words in the cloud (usually 25, unless there were unusually few words co-occuring with s). This choice of scaling equation is ad-hoc, but produces aesthetically pleasing results.

As a point of comparison, the original approach for LyriCloud was to employ a *topic model* such as Latent Dirichlet Allocation (Blei et al., 2003). This is an unsupervised machine learning algorithm that attempts to automatically organize words according to empirical regularities in how they are used in data. Table 2 shows 15 example "topics" induced on the lyrics corpus. Intuitively, these models treat documents (song lyrics) as a probabilistic mixture of topics, which in turn are probabilistic mixtures of words. For example, a religious hymn that employs nature imagery might be a mixture of topics #11 and #13 with high probability, and low probability for other topics (see Blei et al. for more details).

To generate clouds, I trained a model of 200 topics on the lyrics corpus, and let the system choose the most probable topic for a user-provided seed. It then randomly sampled 25 of the 300 most probable words for the corresponding topic, which were scaled in proportion to topic probability. The intuition was that clouds based on the top-ranked words for a topic should be semantically coherent, but sampling at random from a large window would also allow for more interesting and unusual words.

In a small pilot launch of the system, songwriters rejected the topic-based version of LyriCloud for

#	**Most Probable Words By Topic**
1	love baby give true sweet song girl ...
2	la big black white hair wear hot ...
3	hold hand hands head free put back ...
4	love find nothing something everything wrong give ...
5	yeah baby hey man girl rock ooh ...
6	feel make eyes gonna cry makes good ...
7	fall turn light face sun again world ...
8	night day cold long sleep dream days ...
9	mind world lose nothing left gonna shake ...
10	time life long live day end die ...
11	god lord man hell king heaven jesus ...
12	hear play call people good talk heard ...
13	sky eyes fire fly blue high sea ...
14	heart inside pain soul break broken deep ...
15	go back home again time gonna coming ...

Table 2: Example words from a topic model induced by Latent Dirichlet Allocation on the lyrics corpus.

two reasons. First, the top-ranked words within a topic tend to be high frequency words in general (consider Table 2). These were deemed by users to be unoriginal and in violation the first criterion for creativity tools. Tweaking various system parameters, such as the number of topics in the model, did not seem to improve performance in this respect. Second, while words were thought to be coherent overall, users had trouble seeing the connection between the chosen topic and the highlighted seeds themselves (see also the results in Section 3.1). Instead, users wanted to receive interesting suggestions that were more specifically tailored to the seeds they chose, which motivated the information-retrieval view of the problem. While this is plausible using topic models with a more sophisticated sampling scheme, it was beyond the capabilities of a simple PHP/MySQL deployment setup.

3 Results

This section discusses some results and observations about Titular and LyriCloud.

3.1 Empirical Evaluation

I conducted an empirical study of these systems using Amazon Mechanical Turk[3], which is being used increasingly to evaluate several systems on open-ended tasks for which gold-standard evaluation data does not exist (Mintz et al., 2009; Carlson et al.,

[3]http://www.mturk.com

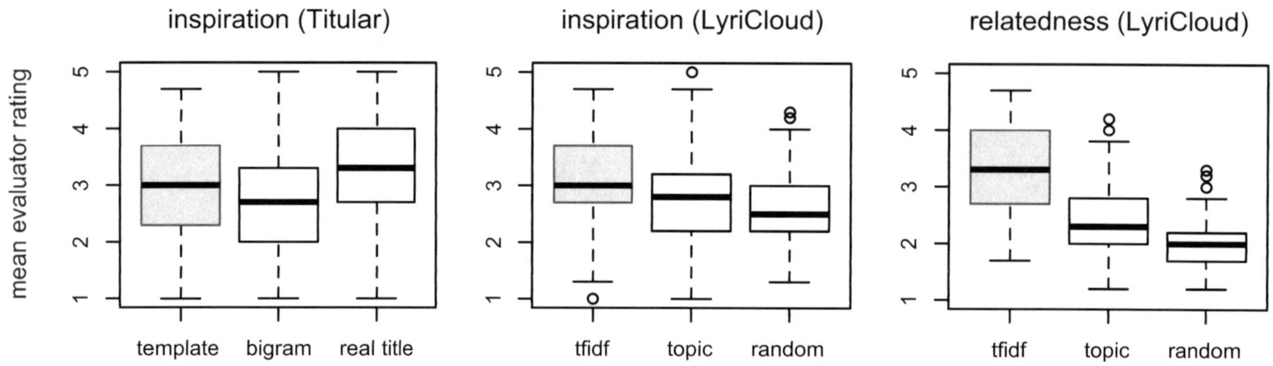

Figure 3: Box plots illustrating the distribution of "inspiration" and "relatedness" ratings assigned by Mechanical Turk evaluators to Titular and LyriCloud output. Boxes represent the middle 50% of ratings, with the medians indicated by thick black lines. Whiskers on either side span the first and last quartiles of each distribution; circles indicate possible outliers. The methods actually deployed for use online are are highlighted on the left of each plot.

Method	Good Title?	Grammatical?	Offensive?
template	68%	67%	6%
bigram	62%	52%	7%
real title	93%	88%	9%

Table 3: Titular results from Mechanical Turk evaluators.

2010). This was done because (1) we would like some quantification of how well these systems perform, and (2) using Mechanical Turk workers should provide more stringent and objective feedback than the songwriters for whom the tools were developed.

For each tool, I generated 200 instances (i.e., titles for Titular and word clouds for LyriCloud) and had evaluators fill out a simple form for each, composed of yes/no questions and ratings on a five-star scale. Each instance was given to three unique evaluators in order to break ties in the event of disagreement, and to smooth out variance in the ratings. Titular is compared against titles generated by a bigram Markov chain model ($n = 1$), as well as actual song titles randomly selected from the lyrics database. LyriCloud is compared against the topic model method, and a baseline where both words and their sizes are generated at random.

Table 3 summarizes Titular results for the yes/no questions in the Mechanical Turk evaluation. At least two of three evaluators agreed that 68% of the suggested template-based phrases would make good song titles, which is higher than the bigram method, but lower than the 93% rate for real song titles (as expected). Similarly, template-based suggestions were deemed more grammatical than the bigram approach and less grammatical than actual songs. Somewhat surprisingly, 12% of all titles in the evaluation were judged to be good titles despite grammatical errors, including "Dandelion Cheatin" and "Dressed in Fast." This is an interesting observation, indicating that people sometimes enjoy titles which they find syntactically awkward (perhaps even *because* they are awkward). All methods yielded a few potentially offensive titles, which were mostly due to violent or sexual interpretations.

Evaluators were also asked to rate titles on a scale from *boring* (1) to *inspiring* (5), the results of which are shown on the left of Figure 3. The template approach does fairly well in this respect: half its suggestions are rated 3 or higher, which is better than the bigram method but slightly worse than real titles. Interestingly, distributional differences between the ratings for template-based output and actual song titles are not statistically significant, while all other differences are significant[4]. This suggests that Titular's titles are nearly as good as real song titles, from an inspirational perspective. Unlike other methods, no single template-based title received a unanimous rating of 5 from all three evaluators (although "The Lungs Are Pumping" and "Sure Spider Vengeance" both received average scores of 4.7).

For LyriCloud, evaluators were asked to rate both the level of inspiration and whether or not they found the words in a cloud to be *unrelated* (1) or

[4]Kolmogorov-Smirnov tests with $p < 0.05$. Multiple tests in this paper are corrected for using the Bonferroni method.

related (5). These results are shown in the center and right plots of Figure 3. In both measures, the *tf·idf* approach outperforms the topic model, which in turn outperforms a random collection of words. All differences are statistically significant. Interestingly, the R^2 coefficient between these two measures is only 0.25 for all word clouds in the evaluation, meaning that relatedness ratings only explain 25% of the variance in inspiration ratings (and vice versa). This curious result implies that there are other, more subtle factors at play in how "inspiring" humans find a set of words like this to be. Additionally, only 36% of evaluators reported that they could find meaning in the size/scale of words in *tf·idf* clouds (compared to 9% for the topic model and 1% for random), which is lower than anticipated.

3.2 Anecdotal Results

The implementations described in this paper were developed over a four-day period, and made available to FAWM participants mid-way through the songwriting challenge on February 16, 2010. They were promoted as part of a suite of online tools called *The Muse*[5], which also includes two other programs, *Struxxure* and *Plot Spline*, aimed at helping songwriters consider various novel song structures and plot constraints. These other tools do not use any language modeling, and a discussion of them is beyond the scope of this paper.

Table 4 summarizes the internet traffic that The Muse received between its launch and the end of the FAWM challenge on March 1, 2010 (thirteen days). Encouragingly, Titular and LyriCloud were the most popular destinations on the website. These statistics include visitors from 36 countries, mostly from the United States (55%), Germany (15%) and the United Kingdom (9%). News of these tools spread well beyond the original FAWM community, as 29% of website visitors were referred via hyperlinks from unaffiliated music forums, songwriting blogs, and social websites like Facebook and Twitter.

FAWM participants typically post their songs online after completion to track their progress, so they were asked to "tag" the songs they wrote with help from these creativity tools as a way to measure how much the tools were being used in practice. By the end of the challenge, 66 songs were tagged "titular" and 29 songs were tagged "lyricloud." Note that these figures are conservative lower-bounds for actual usage, since not all participants tag their songs and, as previously stated, a significant portion of the internet traffic for these tools came from outside the FAWM community.

[5]http://muse.fawm.org

Tool	Pageviews	% Traffic
Titular	11,408	42.9%
LyriCloud	5,313	20.0%
Struxxure	4,371	16.5%
Plot Spline	3,219	12.1%
Home Page	2,248	8.5%
Total	26,559	100.0%

Table 4: Website activity for The Muse tools between February 16 and March 1, 2010. The creativity tools discussed in this paper are italicized.

The tools were published without detailed instructions, so songwriters were free to interpret them however they saw fit. Several users found inspiration in Titular titles that are interpretable as metaphor or synecdoche. For example, Expendable Friend (the stage name of British singer/songwriter Jacqui Carnall) wrote a song around the suggestion "I Am Your Adult," which she interpreted this way:

> So, this is a song about the little voice inside you that stops you from doing fun things because you're not a child any more and you can't really get away with doing them.

Surprisingly, even non-lyricists adopted Titular. "Mexican of No Breakup" led guitarist Ryan Day to compose a latin-style instrumental, and "What a Sunset!" became an ambient electronic piece by an artist by the pseudonym of Vom Vorton.

While LyriCloud was about half as popular as Titular, it was arguably open to a wider range of interpretation. Some songwriters used it as originally envisioned, i.e., a "browser" for interactively exploring lyrical possibilities. New York lawyer and folksinger Mike Skliar wrote two songs this way. He said this about the process:

> I had a few images in mind, and I would type in the key word of the image, which generated other words sometimes slightly related... then kind of let my mind free associate on what those words might mean juxtaposed against

> the first image, and came up with about half the song that way.

Unexpectedly, some took LyriCloud as a challenge to write a song using *all* the words from a single cloud (or as many as possible), since it chooses a seed word at random if none is provided as input. Songwriter James Currey, who actually used LyriCloud and Titular together to write "For the Bethlehem of Manhattan," described the process this way:

> It was like doing a puzzle, and the result is actually quite surprisingly coherent AND good.

As a final anecdote, middle school English teacher Keith Schumacher of California was a FAWM 2010 participant. He shared these tools with faculty members at his school, who designed an in-class creative writing exercise for students involving words generated by LyriCloud, projected overhead in the classroom. This demonstrates the utility of these and similar tools to a broad range of age groups and writing styles.

4 Conclusions and Future Work

In this paper, I introduced the task of designing computational creativity tools for songwriters. I described two such tools, *Titular* and *LyriCloud*, and presented an empirical evaluation as well as anecdotal results based on actual usage during an international songwriting event. I also presented two criteria for creativity tools—that their suggestions be both *unlikely* and *meaningful* to the human artists interacting with them—and showed how these principles guided the development of the tools.

This preliminary foray into creativity tools based on language modeling shows the potential for creativity-oriented human-computer interaction. However, there is still much that can be improved on. For example, Titular might benefit from training with a more traditional context-free grammar (i.e., one with recursive production rules), which might yield more complex and interesting possibilities. LyriCloud could be extended to include bigram and trigram phrases in addition to single words. Also, the vocabularies of both systems might currently suffer due to the limited and domain-specific training data (the lyrics corpus), which could be supplemented with other sources.

Perhaps more importantly, neither of the current tools incorporate any explicit notion of wordplay (e.g., rhyme, alliteration, assonance, puns) or any other device of creative writing (meter, repetition, irony, etc.). The systems occasionally do suggest instances that embody these properties, but they are wholly by chance at this stage. One can, however, imagine future versions that take preference parameters as input from the user, and try to suggest instances based on these constraints.

Acknowledgments

Thanks to Jacob Eisenstein for helpful discussions during the development of these tools, and to the anonymous reviewers for valuable suggestions that much improved the paper. To all the "fawmers" who inspired the project, used the tools, and provided feedback—particularly those who gave permission to be discussed in Section 3.2—you rock.

References

S. Bateman, C. Gutwin, and M. Nacenta. 2008. Seeing things in the clouds: the effect of visual features on tag cloud selections. In *Proceedings of the ACM Conference on Hypertext and Hypermedia*, pages 193–202. ACM.

K. Binstead. 1996. *Machine humour: An implemented model of puns*. Ph.D. thesis, University of Edinburgh.

D.M. Blei, A.Y. Ng, and M. Jordan. 2003. Latent Dirichlet allocation. *Journal of Machine Learning Research*, 3:993–1022.

A. Carlson, J. Betteridge, R. Wang, E.R. Hruschka Jr, and T. Mitchell. 2010. Coupled semi-supervised learning for information extraction. In *Proceedings of the International Conference on Web Search and Data Mining (WSDM)*, pages 101–110. ACM Press.

K. Church and P. Hanks. 1989. Word associate norms, mutual information and lexicography. In *Proceedings of the Association for Computational Linguistics (ACL)*, pages 76–83. ACL Press.

S. Davis. 1992. *The Songwriters Idea Book*. Writer's Digest Books.

K. Deemter, M. Theune, and E. Krahmer. 2005. Real versus template-based natural language generation: a false opposition? *Computational Linguistics*, 31(1):15–24.

M. Farbood and B. Schoner. 2001. Analysis and synthesis of Palestrina-style counterpoint using Markov chains. In *Proceedings of the International Computer*

Music Conference, pages 471–474. International Computer Music Association.

P. Gervás. 2001. An expert system for the composition of formal spanish poetry. *Journal of Knowledge-Based Systems*, 14:181–188.

D. Jurafsky and J.H. Martin. 2008. *Speech and Language Processing*. Prentice Hall.

K. Lari and S. J. Young. 1990. The estimation of stochastic context-free grammars using the inside-outside algorithm. *Computer Speech and Language*, 4:35–56.

T. Li and M. Ogihara. 2004. Music artist style identification by semi-supervised learning from both lyrics and content. In *Proceedings of the ACM International Conference on Multimedia*, pages 364–367. ACM.

H. Manurung. 2004. *An evolutionary algorithm approach to poetry generation*. Ph.D. thesis, University of Edinburgh.

M. Mintz, S. Bills, R. Snow, and D. Jurafsky. 2009. Distant supervision for relation extraction without labeled data. In *Proceedings of the Association for Computational Linguistics (ACL)*, pages 1003–1011. ACL Press.

N. Montfort. 2006. Natural language generation and narrative variation in interactive fiction. In *Proceedings of the AAAI Workshop on Computational Aesthetics*.

Y. Netzer, D. Gabay, Y. Goldberg, and M. Elhadad. 2009. Gaiku : Generating haiku with word associations norms. In *Proceedings of the Workshop on Computational Approaches to Linguistic Creativity (CALC)*, pages 32–39. ACL Press.

R. Neumayer and A. Rauber. 2007. Integration of text and audio features for genre classification in music information retrieval. In *Proceedings of the European Conference on Information Retrieval (ECIR)*, pages 724–727. Springer.

H.R.G. Oliveira, F.A. Cardoso, and F.C. Pereira. 2007. Tra-la-lyrics: An approach to generate text based on rhythm. In *Proceedings of the International Joint Workshop on Computational Creativity, London*.

A. Ramakrishnan, S. Kuppan, and S. Lalitha Devi. 2009. Automatic generation of tamil lyrics for melodies. In *Proceedings of the Workshop on Computational Approaches to Linguistic Creativity (CALC)*, pages 40–46. ACL Press.

C. Solis, J.T. Siy, E. Tabirao, and E. Ong. 2009. Planning author and character goals for story generation. In *Proceedings of the Workshop on Computational Approaches to Linguistic Creativity (CALC)*, pages 63–70. ACL Press.

D. Thompson. 2007. *Hallo Spaceboy: The Rebirth of David Bowie*. ECW Press.

J.M. Yang, C.Y. Lai, and Y.H. Hsieh. 2007. A quantitative measurement mechanism for lyrics evaluation: A text mining approach. In *Proceedings of the International Conference on Business and Information (BAI)*. ATISR.

X. Zhu, Z. Xu, and T. Khot. 2009. How creative is your writing? In *Proceedings of the Workshop on Computational Approaches to Linguistic Creativity (CALC)*, pages 87–93. ACL Press.

Author Index

Association for Computational Linguistics
209 N. Eighth Street
Stroudsburg, Pennsylvania 18360